The Grand Illusion

Unmasked

SG Williams

BSc.(Hons) RAc.

ISBN: 978-1-7775584-9-9

DEDICATION

I am dedicating this book to the many good people who are telling truths and exposing the lies, despite persecution, to make this world a better place.

CONTENTS

ACKNOWLEDGMENTS

I thank my husband for his love, patience, support and
encouragement.

1 PREMISE

Illusion: "... a distortion of the senses which can reveal how the mind normally organizes and interprets sensory stimulation. Although illusions distort the human perception of reality, they are generally shared by most people." - Wikipedia

The world is so full of lies and misinformation it is mind boggling. To try and understand what is really happening is arduous at best. It is no wonder people resort to the simplicity of conspiracy theories. It is not just the attack on truth, it is the escalating armed conflicts, increasing frequency of natural disasters, world-wide polarization of politics and the intentional blurring between right and wrong. It is difficult to know what to do when people no longer have a moral compass that prevents them from boldly shouting lies and denigrating facts in the face of proof to the contrary. Even for those who work to educate themselves on current topics, history and science, are discovering that those things we do consider the hallmarks of truth about the world we live in, are themselves also suspect. Something is off, not right with the world, in a big way. The more we strive to know and the more we learn, the more we realize we know nothing at all.

"The best lies are those wrapped around a core of truth." - Jodi Picoult

Truth now belongs to the loudest and most vocal teller of tales. If they say it long enough, it will be believed. We have been made to feel small and weak and have been conditioned to think this way, since the beginning of civilization. We have been programmed to give our power away to others, who we think are greater and will save us. Puppet masters are even held up for us to follow. Our self-esteem is constantly under attack and if we do speak up and try to do or say anything of value, or worse, be true to ourselves, we are quickly put in our places. The establishment that controls us, will not stand for anyone who knows they are better and more.

All these politics and calls for war and images of disasters are there to distract and demoralize us. However the consciousness of our true selves can override this conditioning and programming. We do not need to be trapped in a hell of our own making nor do we have to keep being reborn to earth, over and over until we get better at avoiding whatever sins we are supposedly committing. Our consciousness and our connection to the spirit of Truth is our ticket to a better place here and now. It is also our way out of this dense unpleasant dimension for all eternity. Just don't let them fool you. Who the "them" is I am not sure.

Many people have an internal barometer of "knowing" that tells them what to believe and what to reject. However can this be trusted? What can we rely on given that even science and experts are no longer considered purveyors of fact? However most of us know the truth when we hear it. We may not be able to understand why we feel the way we do, but many of us have anchors that are unshakable. These come about by what we have learned and experienced throughout our lives. These revelations may be small but over time we see patterns and the pieces we do see, form a picture that gives us clarity. Then those personal truths get validated over and over again throughout our various life events. These are the things we know to be true because we have seen, felt, experienced and tasted it so much, it is a part of who we are. These pillars form the framework for how we judge, learn, discern, fuel and inform our decision making as what we learn from ongoing experiences. In a nutshell this is how we connect to that spirit of Truth.

I am writing this, not to add more conspiracies to

the mix, but to address the herd of elephants in the room. Many of us know, deep down, that there is something very big that nobody wants to talk about. Something is very wrong about everything we have been told about our institutions, our governments, our religions, our world history, who our neighbours are, our place in the universe and who we really are. It feels like more than ignorance, avoidance or over-simplification of facts for convenience, but a deliberate cover up. Many people have had these same feelings. However the world around us, instead of listening, investigating and learning from new revelations, mostly chose instead, to discredit those who have stories and beliefs that don't fit the common narrative. People find themselves rejected, made to feel crazy and vigorously silenced. Continuing to deny the reality of so many, makes people ill, suspicious of those they are supposed to trust and causes them, and those who believe them, to reject those in authority.

Many Truth Tellers have already been exposing the flaws in our historical narratives. The Grand Illusion is the collection of all those shared precepts about who we are, how we got here and why we exist. Because of the explosion of information in this new age, individuals can study and share ideas that were once hidden. As a result, everything we thought we knew is no longer sacred. I have had my own questions about what I have experienced and know to be true, that do not match the common narrative. I need to find, as many of us do, more plausible explanations. Therefore this book will examine many of our accepted stories from a different perspective. Why waste time writing fiction when mining for the truth is so much more bizarre and exciting?

Our humanity and history is much older, richer and more complicated than we can ever imagine. I believe the truth, once realized, would make the greatest story ever told, look boring in comparison. This is a thesis that attempts to find the real truth by unmasking contradictions and fabrications in several different bodies of knowledge. This is a journey of questioning existing, established tenets, finding nuggets of insight, illumination and more puzzles along the way. My hypothesis is that some of the stories we have been told and have always believed to be true, are just part of a grand illusion.

"By doubting we are led to questioning, by questioning we arrive at the truth." - Peter Abelard

However, I should provide a warning. If you find solace in the known world as it is, you may find what I have to say deeply disturbing. I do not expect to be believed nor correct in what I present. These are my findings at this point in my ongoing exploration of ideas. I do stand to be corrected but it would be wrong however, if I could not be allowed to be wrong. I have thoroughly researched my findings to the best of my ability. I am not doing this exercise just for idle interest, but as a serious effort to satisfy myself about what I believe. It is something I am compelled to do for myself. I do believe that my arguments are persuasive and that many of you will, in the end, see what I am seeing.

"The truth is not always beautiful, nor beautiful words the truth." - LaoTzu, Tao Te Ching

2 IN PURSUIT OF TRUTH

"The Truth", Dumbledore sighed, "It is a beautiful and terrible thing and should therefore be treated with great caution". - JK Rowlings from Harry Potter and the Sorcerer's Stone

What is "truth" and does anyone have a monopoly on that? We all have personal biases that tint what we see. It has been said that what we learn from experience depends upon the philosophies and beliefs we bring to that experience. Therefore we are always looking through a periscope of sorts, with limited breath and range. In addition, the human brain does have physical and biological limitations on its capacity for learning and education. As humans there is only so much we can comprehend about the world around us. There will always be unknown frontiers yet to be discovered. Truth is, generally speaking, data that is considered accurate by more than one person based on more than one form of evidential, scientific or expert driven proof. According to Wikipedia:

> *"...Truth involves both the quality of faithfulness, fidelity, loyalty, sincerity, veracity and that of agreement with fact or reality."*

Internal truths are a little different. These are those conclusions that come from personal lessons that have been distilled and separated away from emotional, cultural and physiological biases, desires and wishful thinking. These are the hardest truths to elicit because it is not easy to examine our shadow-selves. Speaking your truth is the public facing self with matching actions and consistent decisions that align with the truth you know about yourself, who you are and what you believe is important. This is the result of an examined, introspective and honest life. It requires work. Full time Truth Tellers must be highly introspective in order to solidify their foundation and not be personally shaken, when the inevitable challenges come.

"Truth Teller" is often synonymous with a straight arrow, upstanding citizen, salt of the earth, an honest Joe and is generally considered to be a good person. Truth Tellers are all these as well as those folks who need to know the facts and feel inclined to do what they can to eke them out. They are inquisitive and interested in what is really happening in order to make sense of what they see. Many feel a moral imperative to be truthful and accurate with others. For some, telling the truth is a part of who they are. However it does not mean that Truth Tellers always tell the truth. Sometimes it is a role played for a particular time, place or situation. Sometimes there are things that a person cannot overlook any longer and lose sleep over, if they do not speak up. I think most of us have been there at some point in our lives.

Truth Teller: The person who regularly brings up the hard issues that others are aware of but not willing to bring forward. The person who isn't afraid to share an unpopular perspective if they feel it is necessary, relevant, or right. - Tony Gambill

Historically, Truth Tellers, the opposite of Liars, come from the Christian and Judaic tradition, having been mentioned in the Old Testament as being a virtuous individual. It was important for some of the kings of old to have at least one person they could rely on, to keep them grounded in reality. In the Bible, the act of telling the truth and the need to refrain from lying, appears as one of the Ten Commandments saying: *"Thou shalt not bear false witness* (perpetuate a lie or false rumour) *against your neighbour"*, Exodus 20:16. In other Biblical books, Timothy says liars and perjurers are considered ungodly, unholy and disobedient to sound doctrine. John calls the devil the *"father of lies"* and equates liars with Satan and evil. Even more harsh is the book of Revelation (21:8) that says:

> *... "as for the cowards... murderers... the immoral...*
> *and all liars, their place will be in the lake burning*
> *with sulphur and fire".*

The majority believe that telling the truth is a quality that we should all aspire to achieve. The reason for that is simple. Lies are deceitful. They mislead people, cause them to err and judge the situation and people in ways that are not helpful. Lies set people up for trouble, disaster and when in the form of negative gossip, is akin to murder. No good comes from a lie. Uncovering lies and liars shines a light on something that can now be repaired or improved. It stops the harm and reveals who to believe and who can be trusted. Truth forms the basis of a stable society where the players follow the rules. It gives everyone a sense of predictability and faith that others will try to do what is right.

However, not all believe lying is a bad thing. Philosophers and other cultural traditions sometimes argue that lying is not immoral. They say that some lies are in fact good and have a place, depending upon the "greater good" and whether the benefits outweigh the harm. Do people ever examine the wider repercussions of their lies? If they did, how could they possibly know where the balance of benefit versus harm falls? Can something that counters a virtue such as honesty, be good? Sometimes, saying nothing and withholding truth may be advantageous, wise and the kindest way forward in some situations. Overly harsh expressions of truth that hurt and demoralize others, can be cruel even if it is for the greater good. However, ultimately, lies rob people of their dignity to be worthy of hearing the truth, it interferes with their free-will to make informed choices and sabotages their choice to affect ethical outcomes. Tolerance of lying is a slippery slope. As people become aware of deceit, they lose trust and become cynical. This leads to a loss of or lack of understanding of the societal rules governing acceptable behaviour toward one another. Ultimately failure to align with truth, can destroy the civility of, and collapse a civilization.

What is the purpose of lies? Often they are a means to distract from the truth, hide it, cover it up and keep things that might be considered bad, a secret. Lies are often used to benefit someone committing a crime or a reprehensible act, who does not want to be punished. Lies often mask something for someone, working in the shadows, who will do whatever it takes, to keep that lie in place. Therefore there is always a danger in speaking up and there are always consequences. Other reasons for lying include:

"... the most common motives for telling lies, avoiding punishment, is the primary motivator for both children and adults. Other typical reasons include protecting ourselves or others from harm,

People who are dedicated Truth Tellers, know there will be negative consequences and prepare themselves accordingly. They continue the path of truth because having a clear conscience, and being able to sleep at night, is of greater importance than any antagonistic outcomes they may have to endure. They know they will become a target and that their own lives will be scrutinized and investigated for any small sin or flaw, in order to be criticized, made un-credible and disbelieved. Those reinforcing the lies, not able to argue intelligently, or too afraid to say anything, will name-call the Truth Teller and launch vicious personal attacks to discredit and invalidate them. Supporters of lies will label Truth Tellers as stone-throwers, agitators, attention-seekers, haters, communists, whiners, traitors, turn-coats, rebels, conspiracy-theorists, radicals, lunatics, as evil or non-human, as reporters of one-sided misinformation, as one of "those" and compare them to the notorious Hitler.

It takes courage to go against the mainstream narrative. Truth Telling should be done carefully and tactfully, with a large amount of forethought, preparation and an understanding of the consequences for everyone involved. Have you thoroughly researched it? Could you be doing it for the wrong reasons? Is it absolutely necessary? Will the benefits outweigh the risks?

"The simple step of a courageous individual is not to take part in the lie... One word of truth outweighs the world." - Aleksandr Solzhenitsyn

Having a good rapport with those around you, understanding them and having their trust, is valuable if you want your words to be taken seriously. Effective Truth Tellers should be motivated by the greater good and infused with caring. The telling should not be done voraciously so as to become brutal and unpalatable. Showing a willingness to be questioned, corrected and asking questions towards a better understanding, goes a long way. It is best done with an eye to furthering the Truth Tellers own information about the matter. At the end of the day, if the urge to speak up continues to return and your own mental wellness is being affected by the silence, then it is something that needs to be done. I also saw a quote (author is disputed) that said *"when Truth Telling, do so with humour and make them laugh, otherwise they will kill you"*.

The Truth Tellers of these last few decades, have been raising red flags and banging gongs to bring attention to the illusions being unmasked in our collective societal reality. Many have discovered new ideas and alternative ways of thinking that raise questions about the validity of what we are told, despite intense opposition from the establishment.

People with different views are being viciously attacked and called conspiracy theorists. According to Wikipedia:

"A conspiracy theory is an explanation for an event or situation that asserts the existence of a conspiracy by powerful and sinister groups, often political in motivation, when other explanations are more probable".

This term has a negative connotation and is often invoked as a way to silence others. It implies that the claimed beliefs stem from prejudice, emotional biases with insufficient reasoning and evidence. However just because it goes against mainstream thinking, does not make it a conspiracy theory. Real conspiracies (*secret plans by a group to do something unlawful or harmful, from the Oxford dictionary*) do exist and the onus is on the believer to provide sufficient evidence for their beliefs. Being called a conspiracy- theorist along with the long list of other derisive names, is often a sign that the Truth Tellers may be touching on, getting close to, or have elucidated the actual and real truth.

There are so many alternative theories currently circulating in the world, that it is overwhelming. Some claims seem preposterous and ridiculous. Some leaders are adamant they are telling the truth when all the hard evidence shows they are not. It is very difficult for anyone to know what to believe anymore.

At this point in our world history, more and more it is up to the individual to determine the truth for themselves. At the very least, it is important for each of us to open our minds, become aware of our misunderstandings, mis-information, inaccurate assumptions, poorly researched opinions, cultural or religious blinders and acknowledge our biases. We should consider and investigate the sources of discomfort we feel with what we hear and use that to inform our knowledge about ourselves.

It is time to question the official versions the authorities are selling. It is important to support and join the rising wave of Truth Tellers. There has never been a time, when the need to get a handle on the truth, has been more urgent than now. In particular, it is time to craft new, more plausible stories about planet Earth and the people that inhabit it. It is time for us to rip the band-aid off everything we thought we knew and take a closer look. Many Truth Tellers are unmasking the Grand Illusion of our times. We need to look inward and do some mental, psychological and spiritual house work, if we want to recognize the truth and understand its significance, when we hear it or uncover it for ourselves.

"An unbelieved truth can hurt a man much more than a lie. It takes great courage to back truth unacceptable to our times..." - John Steinbeck

3 Creation

"Human evolution, at first, seems extraordinary. How could the process that gave rise to slugs and oak trees and fish produce a creature that can fly to the moon and invent the Internet and cross the ocean in boats?" - Steven Pinker

For centuries we have told one similar narrative about our creation and the origins of our species. All the experts say that the universe appeared 13.8 billion years ago. A chemical and physical reaction of elements caused a "big bang" that congealed and cooled, forming the sun, planets and moons. The planet Earth, dated at 4.5 billion years old, was one of these hot masses that eventually gave way to clouds, land masses, lakes and oceans that supported a carbon-based life. The atmosphere, water and elements formed a primordial soup that was seeded with life. Amoebas and protozoan one celled creatures lived and flourished, evolving into mufti-cellular algae, fungi, then swimming fish and mammals that eventually grew limbs to walk the earth. From that large dinosaurs and reptilian animals inhabited the earth until they met with a world-wide cataclysm that changed the climate and created a mass extinction.

We are told that there was a series of climate extremes with temperatures swings from tropical to ice covered, multiple widespread and local flooding, physical upheavals with earthquakes and volcanoes due to tectonic plate movements and several major and minor asteroid collisions, resulting in large and smaller episodes of extinction. Those that survived, went on to further evolve in an explosion of life from plants to animals, reptiles, mammals and birds. Many went extinct and continue to do so, giving rise to the species we see today. Around 6 millions years ago relatives of the apes, chimpanzees and humans appeared. Pressures of natural selection caused apes to become bipedal, finding survival advantages and the ability to out-compete other hominids by remaining upright, eventually evolving into the precursors of modern man, from Homo erectus to Homo sapien, approximately 2 million years ago. Our direct descendants began showing up around 300,000 years ago. There were a number of different species of humans in existence at one time. All of these variations of man, except today's modern version, became part of the genetic mix or died off due to additional climate change and a recent ice age, approximately 12,000 years ago.

Anthropologists and Archaeologists have decided that once the cave dwellers, tool-makers and hunter-gatherers, eventually learned to farm, they no longer needed to be nomadic to follow their food. This enabled them to become stationary. As a result they created communities, towns and villages with governments, division of labour, mass food production, sanitation and clean water systems for populated areas. They created vehicles that enabled them to travel by land and sea, allowing them to spread out from the middle east to the other continents. Complex civilizations first began to emerge in the area of Mesopotamia around 3,000 BC, followed by Egypt, Peru, India, China, the Middle East, Pakistan, Iran and Greece. They formed elaborate partnerships of trading and warring kingdoms with weapons. By 800 BC mankind had established writing, mathematics and religions. Over time, humans had moved from cave dwellers with rudimentary tools to become diverse cultures of people with sophisticated technologies, a wide range of skills, societal rules and laws, elaborate religious practises, artistic temples and several written languages. As storytellers and writers they recorded their experiences, myths and belief systems on stones, in diagrams, on pottery, on papyrus reed, leather and fabric scrolls. Together with the buried remains of their built lives, all these messages and clues were left for future generations to make sense of.

But did we? Does this narrative make sense? I am not sure we know exactly how old the Earth is. Scientists say the Earth is 4.5 billion years old, based on radiometric dating of radioactive elements in rocks. They compare the ratio of parent to child isotopes of radioactive decay to a material with a known, established half-life. Dating the oldest rocks on Earth is problematic because they move, change and get melted back into the Earth's core, on a cyclical basis. Instead scientists compare old Earth rocks to those from the moon and asteroid debris. Age is also determined by where rocks are located in the Earth's horizontal layers of the crust, their relation to other known events affecting the formation of that layer or nearby objects in that same strata of sedimentation. They can examine the magnetism in rocks in the sediment for directionality against the known shifts in the polarity or geomagnetic polarity time scale of the Earth.

Others however attempted to calculate Earth's age using the geothermic rate of cooling of the Earth's core, from complete liquid to the cooled layers we have today. This calculation estimated the Earth to be as young as 24 to 400 million years. That model made some incorrect assumptions that the Earth's core was solid. These estimates have since been retracted. Other young "Earthers" are some who use information from the Bible in a literal manner. They believe Earth to be only 6000 years old. However, such a young Earth could only have been created by magic and supernatural forces if we are to make sense of any of the science, known artifacts and discoveries we have uncovered to date. Therefore understanding how the Earth was created is key.

The Big Bang is the most popular theory of the formation of Earth and other matter in our universe. However it was not a noisy explosion but a very hot dense pin-point of energy-dense mass that quickly expanded, leaving the resulting elements and gasses to cool and congeal. The evidence for this is that we can measure wavelengths of light at the edges of the universe and detect objects still moving outward or expanding. While there is a fair amount of data to corroborate this, there are limitations. For some scientists, the uniformity of background radiation would prove, instead, a steady state universe that had always been expanding. However, the background radiation and composition was found to be changing after all and the Big Bang remains the best theory to date.

That spark of the first life from non-living compounds has been shown to be possible. The right precursor molecules, environmental conditions and input of a source of energy, imitating the conditions that might have been present on early Earth, have been successful in the laboratory by Miller and Urey in 1952. Therefore most believe that life spontaneously erupted from a soup of warm chemicals under optimum conditions. Others believe that the seeds of life may have been planted on earth from other planets by asteroids or meteors. Once life began, however, cells became increasingly complex and evolved into many and varied life forms. It is speculated that the energy that ignited the beginning of all life may have come from lightning, radiation or chemical reactions in the environment.

This haphazard spontaneity of chaos being transformed into a highly ordered, living, breathing, well ordered cycle of life, that supports and is symbiotic with all of nature, does not seem likely. Something seems to be missing because whenever you leave anything alone long enough, without any care, attendance or maintenance, it always falls apart into the smallest components. Just leave something out in the yard long enough, rust, weather and the elements will eventually reduce it to soil. Without an organizing force backed by a huge amount of energy and focus towards order, with a plan (not just a concept of a plan), everything falls into disorder, does it not? Therefore the energy behind that first spark of life and the resulting natural laws and order between such a diverse and interconnection of species we have today, must have been an extremely powerful and intelligent energy.

Darwin's Origin of Species and Theory of Evolution is the generally accepted explanations for how life on Earth came to be. We do see changes and adaptations in species as a response to environmental pressures. This is commonly accepted and can be seen in many examples. We also know that genetic breeding programs will create new variants of species and this is done in agricultural practices all the time. However, although evolution is no longer considered a theory but a fact, it does have two major limitations when used as an explanation for the origin of man. First, there is very little transitional, conclusive and persuasive fossil evidence of the in-between species bridging ape and man. Although man is supposed to have descended from an ape, that missing link is suspect. Scientists cannot agree on any one missing link. There are a number of species of primate that share a few characteristics that make Homo sapiens unique like pelvis contour, hip and knee configuration to enable bipedal walking, brain size, or the shape of the feet or hands. However no one species shares a majority of these. The human evolutionary tree looks more like a bush with loose connections to many different primates.

"The extreme rarity of transitional forms in the fossil record persists as the trade secret of paleontology." - Soren Kierkegaard

The second flaw in the Origin of Species is the timeline. Ancestors of man lived about 6 million years ago, evolving into Homo erectus 2 million years ago. For the Homo sapien direct ancestors of modern man, the oldest fossil remains were found to be about 200,000 years old. This "human" is still considered a species of primate and all the fossils right up to the "links" to humans, still look like apes. After 10 million years apes had been evolving to various shapes and sizes and capabilities but they still all looked "ape-like". The subfamily Hominini containing the genus Homo (for humans) appeared approximately 5 million years ago. Then, it is believed that Homo sapiens evolved from Homo erectus approximately 500,000 years ago. The oldest fossils of modern man, found in Ethiopia, South Africa and Morocco are dated as 200,000 to 300,000 years old. It seems that within a very short window of time, (5% of the total time primates had been on Earth), this planet was covered with a wide diversity of pale to dark skinned, blond to red-haired, blue to brown eyed, hairless modern humans. Furthermore they no longer resemble apes and have far more advanced thinking.

A third conundrum is the question of what happened to the Neanderthals that existed alongside the ancestors of modern humans for anywhere between 3,000 and 5,000 years. They were not the dull witted cavemen as described in popular culture. They lived in small tight communities and were good hunters. Physically they were more robust than us with bigger rib cages, lung capacity, stronger but shorter limbs and strong, fast reflexes. They had a keener sense of smell and hearing with bodies better adapted to the cold. They lived however in a high stress environment competing with large predators for food. They were considered the apex predators however they did incur many injuries due to the risks involved in hunting. Despite being well adapted to the environment and having genes for better immunity than modern man, their lifespans were short (40 years on average) and there was a high infant mortality rate. They had survived previous climate freezes and fluctuation but their extinction was blamed on climate change and in-breeding. They had boats and means of travel but their populations were small. Lack of genetic diversity   brought forward recessive weaknesses expressed as disease and deformities. They did mate with modern humans although this was problematic as some scientists reported findings of sterility in some offspring. Today we still have some of this DNA however their species could have just disappeared into the merging of the two species. In short, despite their natural advantages, natural selection did not work very well for them and the Neanderthals could not make a successful go of life on Earth.

"Like modern humans, Neanderthals probably descended from a very small population with an effective population - the number of individuals who can bear or father children - of 3,000 to 12,000 approximately. However, Neanderthals maintained this very low population, proliferating weakly harmful genes due to the reduced effectivity of natural selection..." - Wikipedia

Evolution and natural selection as the only or single major explanation for the origin of man as having descended from apes, did not work for the Neanderthals and it does not make sense for us. In addition, after the last ice-age of 12,000 years ago, there was a rapid flourishing of the new life we see today. According to my late uncle, a geologist who carbon dated the first sample of moon rock, "most of the species we see today from the geological evidence, just seemed to have shown up all at once".

"To suppose that the eye could have been formed by natural selection, seems, I freely confess, absurd in the highest possible degree." - Charles Darwin (1861). "On the Origin of Species by Means of Natural Selection; Or, The Preservation of Favoured Races in the Struggle for Life", p.167

The Darwinian theory of natural selection and "survival of the fittest", is problematic. Modern man is a misfit in Earth's natural environment. We are too tall for the gravity and it is hard on our spines, our nails and teeth are too dull, we get sick easily, we don't have enough hair on our bodies to keep warm and our eyes and skin are too sensitive for the sun's rays. We don't digest raw vegetable matter very well. It is great for roughage and fibre but the cellulose and lignin is not broken down and we can only manage to extract small amounts of energy and nutrients from it. We do not possess fibre degrading enzymes. Some plants contain material that is toxic to man and most do not have some of the vitamins and amino acids we need. Fruit with available sugars and protein from insects and animals is imperative as is cooking of foods to make nutrients more available and protein safe.

Without the ability to make fire, create clothing, weapons and cook our food, we would be cold, hungry and sick. We are not biologically built with teeth, claws, appendages or speed to capture our prey, We needed to develop tools and methods for hunting and trapping. Without an advanced brain and dexterous hands with thumbs, that have enabled us to find ways to adapt to our numerous shortcomings, we could not survive in nature. So how did we manage to not get eaten and become extinct, before we learned these things. According to scientists we initially did the same kinds of things that the Neanderthals did. Then around the same time the Neanderthal disappeared, about 40,000 years ago, the behaviour of modern man showed signs of an incline in sophistication. Modern man had improved weapons, mined, fished known sources of foods, made beads, created artwork and travelled for trade and exchange of resources.

This level of development was not earth shattering however. Modern man was still behaving and living in a somewhat primitive way for a long time. It seems the real acceleration occurred with the early civilizations where the critical masses and numbers are believed to have fostered need for innovation and ingenuity. It was then that modern man adopted languages, writing, forms of government and acquired advanced knowledge and technologies.

The transition from primitive man to a species that created advanced ancient civilizations is a huge leap. According to Wikipedia: *"Homo sapiens technological and cultural progress appears to have been much faster in recent millennia than in Homo sapiens' early periods. The pace of development may indeed have accelerated..."* This is especially true of a group that needed to first survive and thrive in the natural world before it was positioned to conquer it. Our success could only be explained by an intelligence far beyond that of the Neanderthals. It seems our skeletal frames became smaller, lighter, our muscle mass became weaker and our skulls shrank, as we evolved. Scientists explain this as us getting rid of what no longer served us in our new way of life of city dwelling. If anything mankind is an example of survival of the weakest. Today with all our modern conveniences, few of us would leave home without our creature comforts, cell phones and sunscreen. Our optimal environment is in a sitting position in front of a screen to entertain our minds. Preferably for many, this would be on a comfortable couch with readily available, nutrient deficient sweet and salty, fatty snacks and a diet soda.

"I want to lift the audience to the miraculous in

human nature. After all, we shouldn't be here, with all the odds against us in nature. It's kind of unusual and wonderful!" - Paul Taylor

Those calling themselves Creationists often look at the world as being built exactly how the story of creation is described in the Bible. They are so dedicated to this, that they have waved a magical wand to dismiss the corresponding science that might be applicable. Evolutionists on the other hand, are committed to the materialistic view. Like another form of religion, some clutch their theories, bending the evidence to fit, perhaps not intentionally, but subconsciously because they refuse to admit the involvement of a power higher than science. However, it is hard to believe this entire Creation Story came about by random energy and biological processes alone. This could not just be the result of wonderful dumb luck, a chance chemical reaction that happened once and then cooked itself into an earth stew from which modern man appeared.

The truth, I believe, is the obvious middle ground. Neither party is totally right or wrong when even the scientists who make evolutionary biology their life's work, cannot agree on the story of man. There has to be another explanation for how we came to be. Instead of evolving within nature through natural selection, it is as if we just took ourselves completely out of the "nature" equation. We evolved apart from nature, away from it into a completely separate world of our own. There is nothing natural, ordered or logical about the origins of modern man that fits our scientific theories. Basic chemical and biological processes may have been the methods used but not the mind and power behind the design and execution of it. Anyone that contemplates the beautiful interlocking, intricacies and dynamics of our world, can only be in awe of who or what could have done such a thing.

"For me, the idea of a creation is not conceivable without invoking the necessity of design. One cannot be exposed to the law and order of the universe without concluding that there must be design and purpose behind it all."(also)

"I find it as difficult to understand a scientist who does not acknowledge the presence of a superior rationality behind the existence of the universe as it is to comprehend a theologian who would deny the advances of science." - Wernher von Braun

Someday we will understand how it was done and come up with a better scientific theory than that of evolution alone. This was done over eons of time, using the science we know plus principles of biology, physics, time, energy, dimensions and concepts we don't understand, don't know and have yet to discover. All I can be convinced of is this: We may be descended from primates but in our struggle to survive, somebody(s) with great power, advanced skills, knowledge and technological prowess, intervened to give us weaklings a fighting chance. Somehow, in some way, I feel this was an intentional experiment that was done with forethought, care and a touch of humour.

"I think that many of my ideas are correct, but I'll bet you, before my death other discoveries will be made that will prompt me to alter various ideas I have about human evolution." -Donald Johanson , American paleoanthropologist best known for his discovery of "Lucy"

4 THE ANCIENTS

"Here the artist is, as it were, an archaeologist, uncovering deeper and deeper strata as he works, recovering not an ancient civilization, but something as yet unborn, unseen, unheard, except by the inner eye, the inner ear. He is not just removing apparent surfaces from some external object, he is removing apparent surfaces from the Self, revealing his original nature." - Stephen Nachmanovitch

It is said that civilization began when man stopped nomadic living, hunting, gathering, acquired agricultural practices and formed complex cities. These "civilized", New Stone Age (Neolithic) cities emerged around 12,000 BC after the last great ice age and lasted until approximately 3000 BC. Evidence of these early civilizations is seen in the stone construction of buildings, pottery in art, centralized growing of crops and the domestication of animals.

The culture had grown into complex societies with hierarchies, division of labour, laws, government, industry, trade, organized religion and technological advancements. The evolution of these early civilizations were marked by the use of metals, first copper, then copper alloys during the Bronze Age (3300 to 1200 BC), followed by iron (The Iron Age). Prior to this, the Old Stone Age (Paleolithic) man had used bone and stone to hunt, fish and wild harvest plants while travelling in small groups and living in huts or caves, for 3.5 million years.

The oldest civilized settlements have been said to originate in Mesopotamia inhabited by the Sumerians and others starting around 11,000 BC (13,000+ years ago). Mud was used to make bricks to build city walls, streets, markets, gutters, gardens, homes, towers and temples where the buildings were part of a planned construct. This included the surrounding irrigated agricultural lands and small hamlets. In contrast to these mud-brick cities, at the same time and in the same general region, other establishments had huge multi-ton stone slab stone constructs, giant pillars (mega and monoliths) with pictographs and carved relief of strange animals and unknown symbols. One of these oldest megaliths at Gobekli Tepe, has T-shaped pillars depicting human arms and clothing of men without the heads. The size and precision of these stones, taken from distant quarries, would have been a massive feat to both cut and transport, especially given the tools available at the time. These archaeological sites seem very different in intent and purpose and it is believed that the megalithic sites were temples that the hunter-gatherers were possibly conscripted to build.

Given that Homo sapiens (modern man) came into existence between 500,000 and 300,000 years ago, it took them a very long time, more than 285,000 years of nomadic life, to shift towards urbanization. Then, going forward from 11,000 to 5,000 years ago (3000 BC), we see archaeological evidence that these hunter-gatherers, cave dwelling, pottery makers, had transformed into highly developed social beings with the tools and expertise to create agricultural centres with all the support needed to sustain large populations of people. These early settlements and urban sites show evidence of sophisticated cursive writing, cuneiform text and libraries of literary work. They also reveal developed skills in mathematics, algebra, science, medicine, astronomy, law, religion and philosophy. In a very short time, over a period of only 6000 years, post ice age, mankind seemed to have been enlightened, by knowledge, education and insights, that had been lacking, or so it seems, for a long time.

Even the most knowledgeable, educated and detailed publications, dealing with the development of our civilization, are unpersuasive. The timelines between the unsophisticated nomad and the skilled urban farmers, is too short to be attributed to the linear evolution of man alone. Just as the speed with which it seemed the ape-like humans became smaller, hairless and pale, so quickly, in the big-picture of evolutionary timelines, does not ring true. We know there were many branches of ape-like ancestors and human species like the Neanderthals and the Denisovan. There were also many other species of mammal, reptile and plants that had come and gone over the timeline of the world.

Were there others intelligent beings that either survived or appeared after the last ice age, 12,000 years ago? Our oldest literature, manuscripts and ancient artifacts are full of representations and stories of giants, gods, angels, demons, half-animals, unknown creatures, dragons, unusual people, machines and technology we do not understand. This is just a tiny example of the vast unknown that much of the human race has just assumed are stories of fiction, myth, legend and folklore. But are they? What parts of these stories, if any, are fact or is all of this fiction? They always say that the truth is stranger than fiction and I believe therefore that we have yet discovered the truth of who we are and where we came from.

The existing stories we are told have become increasingly questioned by many experts and lay historians. The more we dig into our past, the more unexplained data is being uncovered. For example, it was only when we began to fly airplanes, that we discovered geoglyph drawings of immense sizes embedded into hillsides. It was only when we ourselves had become more advanced, did we even see the geometric and cosmological characteristics based on the planets and the stars built into the designs of the ancient megaliths. It is only as mankind became more advanced, did we begin to see the intricacies of how the pyramids were built, for example.

"Here is the product of an ancient civilization empowered with the knowledge that as long as the moon continued to orbit the Earth, the special relationship that existed between the two assured the Egyptians of vast amounts of energy. The source of the energy is the Earth itself, in the form of seismic energy. The ancient Egyptians saw tremendous value in this form of energy and expended a considerable amount of effort to tap into it. The benefits they received may have been twofold: energy to fuel their civilization, and the ability to stabilize the Earth's crust by drawing off seismic energy over a period of time rather than allowing it to build up to destructive levels." - Christopher Dunn, The Giza Power Plant: Technologies of Ancient Egypt

We had attributed many of the ancient building sites as having been built by the people whose remains were discovered there by archaeologists and anthropologists. However, as many of the indigenous people of the world have tried to tell us, these built structures were there before they arrived. Now it seems that newer discoveries like that of Gobekli Tepe have made us consider that these civilizations were much older than we thought and that the creation of them by the evolved ape-man was not a realistic explanation. Some have tried to replicate and explain how these structures were built but upon careful scrutiny, it is unlikely that we have the technology, even today, to replicate what was built so long ago. It seems like ancient man had not only suddenly blossomed with an extraordinary knowledge of technology and the heavens, it is very possible that what they knew back then, may be more advanced than what we know today.

"Maui is a beautiful island. It's really the site of an ancient civilization that we've forgotten about, a civilization that existed millions of years ago. When their time came, they left this world and another race was born, the race of human beings." - Frederick Lenz

The world of public opinion has always been divided between what parts of our history is fact and what is fiction. Then as we look at our ancient manuscripts and review the historical myths and legends, we are finding evidence that many of the things we thought were just stories, may have been real. We do know that most cultures around the world have stories of a great flood and we can find geological evidence to confirm this really happened.

We do know dinosaurs existed and that some cataclysmic event must have caused a mass extinction. Today we do have evidence of large asteroid or volcanic events during the time periods in question, that can provide plausible explanations for what happened to those prehistoric creatures. So while some of the stories in the world's collection of ancient texts are believed to be true, much of the other things described are still attributed to fiction. This may not be correct.

It wasn't until recently that we could read the chiselled indentations (cuneiform) made in soft mud and then hardened on walls and tablets in places like Mesopotamia. Many thought that these markings were either a forgotten language or decoration. However, when a wall in Iraq was found to have the same story recorded in three different languages, two known and one in cuneiform, experts were finally able to decipher the chiselled script. Artifacts and tablets that had been stored for two millennia were and are continuing to be, reexamined and translated today. Information on these tablets is providing new insight about past events we did not know about. While the messages are varied, from shopping lists, recipes and to accounting ledgers, for example, there were a number of significant surprises. We learned for example, how astronomers and astrologists, from thousands of years BC, were using complicated geometry and mathematics to calculate the movement of planets. We are now understanding just how sophisticated the people of that time were. Some of the technologies and knowledge they employed were only discovered by modern man in the 1400s.

"The evidence presented by the ancient maps appears to suggest the existence in remote times, before the rise of any of the known cultures, of a true civilization, of a comparatively advanced sort, which either was localized in one area but had worldwide commerce, or was, in a real sense, a worldwide culture. This culture, at least in some respects, may well have been more advanced than the civilizations of Egypt, Babylonia, Greece, and Rome. In astronomy, nautical science, map making and possibly ship-building, it was perhaps more advanced than any state of culture before the 18th Century of the Christian Era. It was in the 18th Century that we first developed a practical means of finding longitude. It was in the 18th Century that we first accurately measured the circumference of the earth. Not until the 19th Century did we begin to send out ships for purposes of whaling or exploration into the Arctic or Antarctic Seas. The maps indicate that some ancient people may have done all these things." - Charles H. Hapgood, Maps of the Ancient Sea Kings: Evidence of Advanced Civilization in the Ice Age

Other tablets from these ancient regions in this area of the Middle East, have stories about gods and rulers that each had a life span of thousands of years. Until the great flood, the longevity of the rulers was immense. Gilgamesh was a giant part-god, part-man who is mentioned in apocryphal (non accepted) Biblical books. He was said to have been 7 feet tall and ruled for 126 years. While assumed to be a mythological story, Gilgamesh is listed on the cuneiform block called the Sumerians Kings List, suggesting he was a real historical figure. The Epic of Gilgamesh, the oldest literature known (4000+ years old), has many stories that mirror the stories in the Bible. It is thought that perhaps this text formed the basis for many Biblical books. The difference is however that the Epic of Gilgamesh is about the adventures of several "gods" and people with great powers, where the Biblical text replaces the names for the "gods" with only the One Almighty God.

All cultures around the world have ancient texts alluding to the same shared common stories. The gods of the Greek, Roman and even Norse pantheons were mythical stories of heroes with both human weaknesses and god-like powers. The Chinese culture's ancient religions of Taoism also supported the belief in similar super-humans who were divine and immortal. From this we have a repeating echo that exists until this day of having geographically separate areas of groups of people, mortals or peasants, led by or overseen, even owned by, rulers, kings or lords who were divine, divinely appointed or equivalent to gods. Humans have always believed in something bigger and more powerful than they. It is as if we have been programmed to be servants-to, slaves-of a different, better elite group. This kind of thinking has been baked into the entire history of our world.

In addition to the known insights from archaeological records and Sumerian texts, Gobekli Tepe and other similar sites in Turkey, the Nag-Hammadi library and the release of the Dead Sea scrolls found at Qumran, have uncovered previously unknown ancient papyrus scrolls and codex "books". More texts have also been found or unearthed in archaeological libraries and private collections. Many of these works are giving us very different stories of our ancient history than we had before. The recent findings have confirmed that civilized man is older and more sophisticated than we thought.

Other texts have confirmed that many of the books used in the Christian Bible are valid with even older versions of the same books now showing up in the scrolls. However, there are many other texts that provide a different view of early Christianity than we have been told previously. It seems that there had been a much broader interpretation of the teachings of Jesus between his disciples who did not agree with one another. Some of the lost gospels were hidden over a period of years as councils of Bishops and church leaders disputed the details. While Jesus himself is considered both the Son of Man and the Son of God by every sect (including non-Christian religions), they could not agree on the degree of god-ness versus man-ness. Some religions that exist today still say he was an enlightened man but only human, while others say he was God incarnate and his human aspect was just a guise.

Some people today even wonder if Jesus was a mythological figure? However the overwhelming evidence of the ancient gospels, attributed to those who knew him, say he lived and was crucified. Critics however suggest that these writings may have been the result of Christian interpolation whereby church authorities altered the text. Many say that the Talmud also mentioned Jesus by the name of Yeshua (pronounced in Arabic as Yeshu) but this is still under debate. In addition, there are credible non-religious ancient historians that say Jesus lived and was crucified during the period of time in question. One was a Roman-Jewish historian known for his fact checking, another a Roman lawyer in his letters to Roman authorities, another a stoic philosopher's letter to his son, a second Roman historian in his treatise of the Caesars of that time and a number of minor Greek and Roman sources. Therefore based on objective evidence, we do know Jesus did exist and was crucified. However there is and was much dispute over who he was.

Is it possible that gods and god-man hybrids did or do exist on Earth? Jesus has been given the attributes of God with much documentation to claim he performed many miracles. This lends much credence to him having extraordinary abilities of some kind.

We are also pretty sure that Gilgamesh was real and that he too was said to have god-like and super-human qualities. Then people who are experts in Biblical translations are now telling us that many of the different names for God in the Old Testament are not that at all. These are all different "gods" who ruled over distinct geographical groups of people. We know even based on science that there were many species of Hominids at the time Homo sapiens emerged. Some were dwarf-like while others were giants that are presumed to have gone extinct. The Bible itself tells stories of super-human beings and of giants like Goliath. The Books of Enoch, approved in the Ethiopian Bible, tell us a fantastical story of beings coming to earth and mating with humans to form god-men. That man was also given advanced knowledge and technologies by some of these gods. More and more we are uncovering evidence that these were not just myths.

According to the Maoshing Ni version of the *Yellow Emperor's Classic of Medicine (The Neijing),* written more than 2200 years ago, there were four types of ancient peoples that existed on earth a long time ago, that lived very long lives and did not display the usual signs of aging. The Immortals lived the longest, followed by the Sages, then the Achieved Beings and lastly the Naturalists who lived to over one hundred years:

"The immortals kept their mental energies focused

and refined, and harmonized their bodies with the environment. Thus, they did not show conventional signs of aging and were able to live beyond biological limitations."

"...Not so long ago (the)... achieved beings, who had true virtue, understood the way of life, and were able to adapt and to harmonize with the universe and the seasons. They too were able to keep their mental energy through proper concentration... These achieved beings did not live like normal human beings, who tended to abuse themselves. They were able to travel freely to different times and places since they were not governed by conventional views of time and space. Their sense perceptions were super-normal, going far beyond the sight and hearing of ordinary human beings. They were also able to preserve their life spans and live in full health, much as the immortals did."

"...there was a third type of person, known as the sage. The sages lived peacefully under heaven on earth, following the rhythms of the planet and the universe... The sages lived over one hundred years...A fourth type were natural people who followed the Tao and were called naturalists. They lived in accordance with the rhythmic patterns of the seasons: heaven and earth, moon, sun and stars. They aspired to follow the ways of ancient times... They too, lived plainly and enjoyed a long life."

Given   the timelines of man's explosive and impressive appearance on the world stage of ancient civilizations, the advanced knowledge and the stories we assumed were myths, but most likely aren't, makes the stranger story more probable than what we have been told. It is perceivable that until now, we did not understand enough to know that we didn't know. It is also expected in the way man and his ego has always thought of himself as special and at the center of the universe. We like to think we are unique but the more likely truth is that we are not alone in this vast universe. Given all the evidence, it is a real possibility that we are descendants of genetically modified, part-god, advanced higher beings. As depicted in many artifacts found at ancient archaeological sites, the Ancients that inhabited our world were most likely highly intelligent, knowledgeable beings who created hybrids of men, of animals and strange beings we are loath to imagine. If we are going to find out the truth, we need to reexamine everything we have been told. Therefore there are a few haunting questions that remain: "Who were these Ancient beings?", "What role did they have in the history of man?", "Why did they leave?" or "Did they?". Could it be possible that this new understanding and perspective on reality is the *"truth, that is stranger than fiction"*? I think so.

5 Extra-Terrestrials

"For me, it is far better to grasp the Universe as it really is than to persist in delusion, however satisfying and reassuring." - Carl Sagan

It is one thing to understand who we are in terms of our creation and the development of human civilization, but where do we fit in the larger picture of the universe? This is an area that is still under immense speculation, ridicule and debate. This is also a subject that has been a target of cover-ups and denial by experts and authorities even more than any of the other topics I have already discussed. As a human race, it is possible that we have been the subject of manipulation by altered, hidden or false information for most of our existence on earth. This statement can only come from a conspiracy theorist, one might argue, where the label negatively denigrates the opinion holder to someone unreliable.

A conspiracy is simply a secret agreement, plot or plan between individuals usually inferred to be something illegal or bad. A conspiracy theory is simply the explanation of a situation or event based on a conspiracy. Conspiracies do exist and to point out the real evidence of such, does not make one a crazy theorist but a truth-teller or whistle-blower.

The belief in ETs, life on other planets and the visitation of aliens to the planet Earth is one such event or situation, that experts and those in authority, refuse to openly acknowledge. There are many stories of such unexplained encounters reported by reputable people. However often, those who report these sightings, are made to feel like they are not believed and that something is wrong with them. Official reports of such observations, even by authorities, have historically been classified. It has been reported that over a 22 year period in the recent 20th century, there were 12,000 official records of strange phenomenon by one secret project of American scientists, alone. In my own small corner of the world, from 1950 to 1997, Don Leger's book, *Maritime UFO Files*, lists 81 reports of UFOs (Unidentified Flying Objects) now called UAPs (Unidentified Anomalous Phenomena), mysterious events, encounters and even abductions from personal accounts, military and RCMP documents. This may be just the tip of the iceberg. Historical records of encounters go back over 3000 years. Given most people do not report these traumatic events for fear of being ridiculed or having to relive something very upsetting, this number is likely much higher.

When so many modern accounts of UAPs are voiced, denying the truth of the existence of ETs and their contact with Earth, is a real conspiracy. The question however is, "who is doing the cover-up and why"? Most scientists today will agree, given the size of our universe and the huge number of planets, the chance of the existence of other habitable planets like Earth and life on other planets, is probable. Some say the denial and concern is a matter of security and safety. However, given the evidence of advanced technologies, if the aliens wanted to harm us, there would have been some indication of that by now. There is no evidence, at least that I know of, that beings from other planets are planning to annihilate us. It is more likely that the secrecy is there to protect the information that they have already captured alien life and technologies. Such governments are trying to reverse-engineer their findings in order to gain a financial and weapons advantage over other nations, out of the lack of trust and a preponderance of greed.

The fact is however, that a project to check into the decades long issue of possible ET contact was initiated in the United States to get to the bottom of the question. During Project Blue Book, scientists examined reports and claims up to the current observations at that time (1969). Then again early in 2024, the Pentagon announced that the Defence

Department's AARO (All-domain Anomaly Resolution) office's investigations of reported sightings going back to 1945, found no evidence of aliens. This was surprising given the many claims world-wide of people who had experienced unexplained phenomena. It is frightening to experience something that challenges your sense of reality. Then to be questioned, disbelieved and have your reputation and sanity questioned and marred for the rest of your life, is not something anyone would welcome. Most people do not choose to be terrorized and would not report the experiences unless they believed they were true. They would most likely feel the need to warn others and initiate an investigation for the welfare of everyone. These are not experiences most people would make-up or seek out.

In addition, these are also not experiences of just individuals but many have seen the same things at any given event. Plus sightings of UAPs are often corroborated by parties of others from different locations on the ground, by radar and often by military or police authorities. These reports are often supported by a number of responsible and credible witnesses. Therefore the idea of possible visitation from aliens is not just the wild imaginings of individuals or a form of mass hysteria. Even credible scientists over the years have agreed that the likelihood of alien presence was probable. Our ancestors certainly believed in other-worldly beings from past stories, legends and writings. Even one of the most widely read collections of books, the Bible, has a few passages that refer to beings and technology that we now know would have been ETs and space craft.

In *Genesis* chapter six, heavenly beings that were immortal, took a liking to some of the human women they found to be beautiful and mated with them. Giants were created from these unions. Also other powerful beings, who were part god and man, became great heroes of the legends of long ago. God was not happy about the evil ways of his creation and decided to wipe them all out (save Noah who himself it seems was a hybrid god-man, or at least the son of) in the great flood and start over. In *Genesis 28: 12*, Jacob "dreamed" of a stairway of light stretching between earth and heaven with angels going up and down. Elijah in *2 Kings*, chapter two, is taken up into heaven in a whirlwind by a fiery chariot pulled by horses of fire. He departed Earth without having died. *Ezekiel* chapter one, describes creatures with four heads, wings and hands moving in a square formation, shining like bronze. There were four wheels, with wheels, within a wheel, moving in four directions, shining like a precious stone and making the sound of a roar when in flight. With this there was also a blazing torch, shooting flashes of lightning darting back and forth with great speed originating from a shining crystal dome that reached overhead. Inside there was a human figure on a throne made of sapphire, shining with bright light and colours of the rainbow.

These are just a few examples of passages from widely known texts. However the books of *Enoch* in the Ethiopian Bible, ancient Sumerian texts, Dead Sea scrolls and literature found at Nag-Hammadi, also point to the existence of other worldly beings. The books of *Enoch* expand upon the passage in *Genesis* by describing in detail the acts of the sons of heaven (the angels called Watchers) in taking up with the daughters of men and the resulting giants. These Watchers also taught the humans the secrets of charms, enchantments, metal work, weapon making, makeup, dying, reading of the clouds, signs of the planets, the moon and many other things the humans were not supposed to know. The ancient Sumerian texts and *The Epic of Gilgamesh*, talks about a group of large, powerful deities called the Anunnaki that were the offspring of the gods of heaven and goddesses. Also described were lesser gods that performed labour for the Anunnaki who eventually revolted, asking for help, upon which humans were created to be that help.

In a similar way the mythologies of the middle east (those of Hittites) evolved into the Titans and Olympians of Greece and Rome. These same themes can be found all over the world in every culture. The Tuath De, are the gods and goddesses in Irish mythology, with various roles, who interact with humans, have supernatural powers, do not age and can shape shift. The Chinese people see themselves as the descendants of the Yellow Emperor and the Dragon. They believe this emperor flew to earth in a craft and they celebrate this with a Yearly Dragon Dance. Mayan and Inca tales from South America are full of deities, heroes and superheroes. Indigenous non-European cultural practices are closely tied to the belief in ETs.

Ancient Egyptians believed their rulers to be the incarnation of Horus that linked the human and spiritual world. It was discovered in the last century that there were differing physical characteristics between the ruling class and their followers. Examined remains showed larger skeletal structure and cranial capacity of the rulers. Even the burial artifacts, architecture and the style and content of paintings on walls changed around 3000 BC, suggesting that Egypt was taken over by a different race, possibly from Mesopotamia. This conquering foreign elite seemed to have accelerated the technological advancements of what was still a primitive society at that time. A pharaoh called Akhenaten, possibly the father of King Tut, from around 1300 BC, called himself a god-king and iconographical pictures show him as having a distinctive cone shaped or elongated skull and feminine, androgynous body features. The skull shape was confirmed in the last century by examining a tomb believed to be his.

Other rulers were also found to have a cone shaped skull. Khinglia, of the Alchon Huns, another god-king, is depicted as having a steeple shaped head like the Alchon people he ruled. These people inhabited southern Russia, Afghanistan, Pakistan and India. It seems that this cranial abnormality has been found in ancient burial sites all over the world. A researcher studying the elongated skulls of the Paracas in Peru, determined that not all cone shaped skulls were artificially induced. Some of these skulls had a larger volume than normal, the hole where the spine entered was smaller, more oval and further back than a normal human skull. Also the suture lines where the skull bones fuse together after birth were 2 instead of 3. In addition there are 4 holes in the skull face (foreman for facial nerve and blood vessels) that were missing but instead were located on the top-back of the elongated skull. Infants of these cone shaped beings were also born with a full set of teeth.

A doctor examining these skulls from Paracas in Peru, determined that these were not human abnormalities but normal features of a different species. These differences were not within the normal spectrum of human variation. These were also not artificially induced cranial abnormalities. These elongated skulls were also found in Egypt where the artificial shaping of the skulls was not a common practice in ancient times. This condition was a normal genetic familial characteristic, proven by the finding of an Egyptian fetus, enclosed in the mummy of a pregnant woman, with the same cone shaped head. DNA testing of these skulls showed that they had originated from the region now known as Turkey. These elongated heads are historically associated with the ruling classes in many cultures and are also found in common with the ancient and highly sophisticated ancient megalithic archaeological sites. Were these the gods that mixed with the human race and caused the spike in man's knowledge, learning and evolution? The artificial cranial deformation practices may have been man's way to enhance social status and identify with these more noble races.

Were indeed these non-humans a race of people that came from other places in our universe? Were they among the angels and giants that were seen in ancient skies and that drew astrological maps on the earth and that built technology we do not understand. Ancient humans would not know how to describe shiny metallic flying machines and their heat propulsion systems in any terms other than what they knew, fiery dragons and shining chariots with wings. Modern man has reported alien-like phenomena for centuries. Many accept Christ in Christianity as both God and human. Ancient artifacts, petroglyphs and carvings on sarcophagi, all over the world, from many cultures, show us scenes that look distinctly like spacemen and spacecraft. The more we discover, the more we see a picture of a people with far more knowledge, skills and technology than they should have had. Some of these artifacts we still do not understand.

Therefore why do experts stifle this knowledge and suppress the findings? Why do "they", "we" and our governments vehemently deny the existence of, and our interactions with, "Aliens" or ETs? Canada has made it known in 2023 that it has an official UAP (Unidentified <u>Aerial</u> Phenomena) study called Sky Canada Project that was launched in 2022. It promises to be more open, is collecting information from other Canadian offices, other countries and claims to support citizen science. However it is not intended to collect first hand accounts and the mandate is not to prove or disprove the existence of Aliens. It seems it is there to facilitate the collection of observations and report back to Canadians. Canada did have a couple of projects in the 1950s that collected observations of UFOs at the time, but they were disbanded saying that the investigations did not lend themselves to scientific study. However, one of the studies by senior engineer Wilbert Smith with Transport Canada concluded, after looking at data and reports, *"that UFOs were ET (Extra-Terrestrial) in origin and used the manipulation of magnetism to fly the object or craft"*.

It seems that this is an area that can no longer be ignored. What is clear however is that this is a topic of extreme sensitivity with information being highly filtered and suppressed. Reporting an ET or UAP encounter is still riddled with stigma and ridicule, although this has improved somewhat. It helps that high profile people are speaking up about their experiences and that people with high ranking positions in the military and former military, are admitting that ETs are real. I see that the Sky Project's promised report for this year is not yet released. I am still skeptical and hope this is not just another cover-up campaign. I will believe the new position of transparency, only when I see the resulting report. As stated on the government website, it is expected in the fall of 2024.

When the US's AARO provided their 2024 investigative report on UAPs, going back to 1945 and reported that there was no evidence of "aliens", perhaps they were correct. Maybe it was not aliens that they found but ETs that were human like us. So technically they were correct in their report using these semantics. However, I believe instead they found evidence of unusually advanced humans and their technologies, not just extra-terrestrials but intra-terrestrials, both hidden and walking among us. Perhaps what they actually found was evidence of our relatives whose evolutionary journeys were much longer than ours and with lineages that stretched back to forgotten times on Earth, or elsewhere. Not only are we not alone as the only humanoid species on Earth, we probably never were. In fact ETs are most likely our cousins and we have family members with a much broader variety of shapes, sizes, colours, textures, abilities and temperaments throughout the entire cosmos.

"We are not alone in the universe. A few years ago, this notion seemed far fetched; today, the existence of extraterrestrial intelligence is taken for granted by most scientists. Even the staid National Academy of Sciences has gone on record that contact with other civilizations "is no longer something beyond our dreams but a natural event in the history of mankind that will perhaps occur in the lifetime of many of us." - Lambros D. Callimahos, Communication with Extraterrestrial Intelligence released by NSA 2004

***

"A former Canadian defence minister (Paul Hellyer) is heading a speaking tour about the alleged cover up of UFOs by world governments... Hellyer and the other speakers on the tour want the government to release all the information they have on UFOs. (He) ...first spoke out about his belief that governments are covering up an alien presence in 2005. He says "UFOs are as common in our skies as airplanes"... (He also says) "Much of the media won't touch it," he told CTV Calgary. "So you just have to keep working away and hope that someday you get a critical mass, and they will say, in one way or another, 'Mr. President or Mr. Prime Minister we want the truth and we want it now because it affects our lives.'"

6 ROLE OF BELIEF

"Most contemporary philosophers characterize belief as a "propositional attitude"... the mental state of having some attitude, stance, take, or opinion about a proposition or about the potential state of affairs in which that proposition is true.." -Stanford Encyclopedia of Philosophy

As far back as you can go, ancient people have always held a collective belief in gods with supernatural powers. The Greeks, Romans, Egyptians, Celtic and Indigenous people have detailed stories and accounts of other worldly folks, They have described spirit realms with whom we could communicate and travel to. Shaman of every culture are specialists that know how to connect to the invisible worlds. Man has always searched for and has believed in something bigger. Most cultures believe in something unseen, a powerful invisible force that connects us with everything, both in the present material world and in the afterlife.

Belief systems have always been the foundation for most cultures to help us understand the laws of nature, the origins of the universe, man's purpose and how to make sense of life on earth. In the earliest mythology, the cornucopia of gods resembled super-humans with traits similar to man. Later religions evolved to help man achieve spiritual oneness with the universe. Some through spiritual practices of meditation. Others through faith in one God. In general, almost all the world's belief systems include, life after death, angels and demons, good and evil and a powerful, omnipotent, benevolent creator, higher power and or life force as core tenets.

Yes, there are many people who do not believe in any sort of unseen world. What you see is all there is. Even for those who claim to be an agnostic or atheist, it should be hard to overlook man's obsession with the invisible, fantastical, dimension to normal life. Just look at the many popular movies with witches, vampires, wizards, zombies and superheroes as the main theme. Also noteworthy are books like *Lord of the Rings*, *Harry Potter* and TV shows like *Dr. Who* and *Star Trek*. Even those who do not believe in a higher power, may have occasionally been inclined to explore the possibility that supernatural beings, multiple dimensions of reality and magic might exist.

If things are not as they seem, what is real and why does it seem like we live in an alternate reality of sorts, or do we? Many people who have questioned the nature of what we believe about our world, say yes. This medium we find ourselves living on and in, is not real. Some early pioneers included *Chariots of the Gods?* author Erich von Daniken. He looked at megalithic architecture, artifacts, geoglyphs and questioned if these presented evidence of ancient astronauts. David Icke, a former BBC sports broadcaster and author of 20 books, had spiritual experiences that led him into a lifetime of research. His findings continue to evolve but he is convinced that the reality we see is equivalent to a massive computer game being manipulated and controlled by groups of puppet humans and beings more intelligent than us. Another pioneer was radio broadcaster and author, Art Bell, who hosted a number of talk radio stations where he introduced to the world the opinions and ideas of experts in UAPs, psychic phenomenon, near-death experiences and alleged secret military projects. These folks helped to pave the way for more people to question human history and experience.

At the same time there were pioneer philosophers, shamans and eastern religious gurus that had always believed that there was something bigger and something more to mankind. Alan Watts, a professor and author on Zen philosophy, taught that we are the "all there is" and that man's struggles are like a game of hide and seek with the divine, where we are hiding from ourselves. That our perception as humans (egos in a bag of skin) is a myth and we have forgotten who we really are. Carlos Castaneda was an anthropologist and author that showed us the inside journey of a shaman, that he himself supposedly walked as a mentee of a Yaqui "Man of Knowledge". He showed us that man still has the ability to see and be connected to the unknown non-ordinary reality. Richard Alpert (Ram Dass) was a psychology professor, spiritual teacher and author who introduced the western world to eastern philosophies. He inspired many people to seek a spiritual path of consciousness, and the "something more" in the here and now of what is possible. These pioneers all had views that challenge our perceptions of self, mankind and our accepted world reality. However they were also a thorn in the side of those powers and principalities who wanted to maintain the accepted story lines.

"We tend to accept information that confirms our prior beliefs and ignore or discredit information that does not. This confirmation bias settles over our eyes like distorting spectacles for everything we look at." - Kyle Hill

Our beliefs need to be updated with continuous learning. In addition, our methods of learning can be flawed in very subtle ways that affect how we perceive the world around us. Do we make assumptions about a situation we experience because we already "think we know" or are too polite to ask questions? The result is that we don't learn anything new but instead reinforce what we already "think we know". This endless cycle or "loop" keeps us spinning in the same thinking (loopy-thinking). There is also conditioned-thinking, when we have been programmed to react and see things in a specific way, through the lens of our upbringing, cultural and other biases. Therefore our state of mind and what we already believe, affects learning and our ability to shift our beliefs. According to C.S. Lewis:

"What we learn from experience depends upon the philosophy we bring to that experience."

The pioneers already mentioned and many more, have had a profound impact on the thinking and ideas of the last century. Their paths were made difficult by many of the influencers of their day who did everything to discredit them both personally and professionally. To this day their books and ideas are still widely popular and the ones that are still alive (von Daniken and Icke) are still writing and speaking to large audiences. Do we just write them all off as quacks? Unfortunately that is usually what most of us do when people say things we don't like. Some of these pioneers may have gotten a few things wrong but if you listen carefully, some of what they say may be right. Nobody gets it all right, all the time. We are all in a process of continual learning. However a wise person can consider the views of their opponent, benefit from another perspective and find nuggets of truth. This is the kind of discernment that involves the spirit, the heart, along with reason and reflection as we make sense of our own experiences and the significance each event has, in our own lives.

"It's not the events of our lives that shape us, but our beliefs as to what those events mean." - Tony Robbins

Famous writers and spiritual teachers like Deepak Chopra, Eckhart Tolle, Wayne Dyer, Sadhguru and psychologists like Phil McGraw have acquired cult followings for their insights into what it means to be human. For centuries people of many religious faiths have gone on pilgrimages to their revered sacred sites. The search for enlightenment is growing especially as the world becomes more polarized. So too, the voice of fanaticism seems to be growing louder as people attempt to simplify the world into black and white. Legalistic thinking fuels emotion, not just in regard to faith but in politics and nationalistic loyalties.

Why is that? And why is it that over the history of the world, beliefs organized into religions have spawned so much passion in people, that it created human suffering and war? Faith in a higher power or a belief system, runs far deeper in man, than intellectual ideas or philosophy. It has an irrational depth of emotion attached to it. The recurring theme of good versus evil is ubiquitous. It is a guttural knowledge that sits in the core of one's being. Sometimes even the mind has difficulties reconciling and explaining it. Has the quest to "know the truth", to seek "one's purpose in life" been programmed into our DNA? It does seem that this is an instinctual behaviour not seen in other animals.

It is said we differ from animals in that we have complex speech, more powerful reasoning, analytical skills and problems solving abilities. However, it can be said that some animals also show signs of this in the language of dolphins, reasoning of elephants and the problems solving of crows for example. What does seem to set us apart is our emotions and the penchant for introspection and creativity. The most striking characteristic of humans is the development of the ego that instills a self-consciousness that makes us think we are separate from others and nature. This feeling of being a unique separate entity and alone, in a world filled with like-others, is a unique human trait.

I do not believe that animals judge their world based on right and wrong, good and evil. They just exist harmoniously with nature. Why can't we do that? The reason is, I believe, that we have forgotten who we are. Some young children do remember but over time this is conditioned out of them as the education system teaches us about a world we are supposed to see. Teenagers especially struggle between conscious knowing and the growing spectre of the subconscious ego. They still dimly see the dichotomy between who they thought they were, what they believe about the world and who others say they are. Then in adulthood, the busyness of getting on with daily life and survival, forces them to forget the philosophical struggle, move on and make the best of life as they know it.

One method of reversing the loss of curiosity and child-like wonder and getting to the truth of one's reality, is to go back and recapture the memories of a time when every bug and little flower was a beautiful thing. Each person has a time in their lives before their innocence is corrupted. The purpose is not to lament the things that cost us our youth, but to find that magic again, move forward and reconcile the war between reason and longing. Some find this in religion or meditation by discovering a higher power and/or that power within themselves. Forgiveness, letting go of the past and accepting all our historic events as necessary lessons in life, helps us move forward. Allowing yourself to let go and relax into the present moment where everything is OK, is one way to move towards that state of wonder.

Internal discomfort and longing however, seems to have a purpose. It nudges us to reconnect with the supernatural and natural world where good and evil are both necessary polarities. It helps us find a path towards internal and external harmony. Rather than burying it in work, pleasure and endless activity, the tension is there to get our attention. It is there like our consciences to force us to take a look at ourselves. It is there to help us discover that despite all the struggles, we are managing to survive and that we will be OK, no matter what happens. It is there to help us realize that the universe does care for us just as it does the flowers and the birds.

In order to reclaim that wonder, we also need to seek out and come to terms with what we believe about the invisible realm. We have to figure out what we will accept and what to reject. This is a pilgrimage one must take by facing the tough questions head on. Who am I? Why am I here? Is there a God or higher power? Is there life after death? Each individual must come to their own realization that they are not separate and do belong as an integral, important and splendidly beautiful part of the universe, complete with all the good parts and bad bits, just as they are. In this space, one can reclaim the freedom of spirit, wonder of youth and the ability to recognize, discern and know "what is truth" when it matches the truth we know from our connection to the universal, spiritual, all knowing realm.

What we believe and the journey toward finding out what that is, is a critical component in the determination of our future path. Belief directs our thoughts, actions and behaviours. It can be a form of internal illumination, like a mini-superpower. It can also behave as a dark cloak of constraint and a crippling weakness. We gravitate toward and manifest those things we hold deeply in our beliefs. That is why it is most important to know, at a subconscious level, those solidified positions of perspective that reside within us. Even those ideas we would never question, about who we are and the world we are in, will inform and instruct the direction of our life even without our conscious permission or knowledge. Our powers can work against us if we do not make them known, conscious and available to the mind and intellect. Our source of power can help us if we ensure our beliefs are good, true and and synchronous with our actions.

"The thing always happens that you really believe in; and the belief in a thing makes it happen." - Frank Lloyd Wright

Signs of what is happening in the world are all telling us it is time to emerge from the cages of the old ideas. We need to begin, or continue, to question the norms, customs, expectations and beliefs that others impose on us. The alternative sources of knowledge tell us that we are not only inextricably connected to our physical environment, as science outlines in quantum physics, but we are also one with the invisible consciousness of the universe. Therefore our thoughts and actions not only affect our own health but the well-being of others and how the future is manifested. We need to prepare our hearts and souls for change. It is not easy to be who you really are. It is especially hard to break away from the constraints family and friends put on us, to be who they think we are, and should be.

We need to be the light that will guide the world and expose the darkness, the falsehoods and lift the fog of this world to show the truth for what it is. Our beliefs are often that veil that blocks our vision and will not allow us to see the truth clearly. Our beliefs are like wearing a mask with the cut outs for the eyes, being just a bit too small. We need to examine all the ways we are constrained from seeing our reality for what it is. Belief comes with a multitude of assumptions that need to be examined in order to shine light on the world. Our beliefs therefore, are critical to what we are able to learn and perceive, if we are able or willing, to see and accept the truth of ourselves and the universe, and whether we will succeed both as an individual and as a human race.

"Remember, we see the world not as it is but as we are. Most of us see through the eyes of our fears and our limiting beliefs and our false assumptions." - Robin S. Sharma

7 Religion

"The concern is not with an academic or intellectual understanding of our religions, rather, our focus is the experiential path of the individual as it reflects the key revelation of our enduring religions." - Bernadette Roberts

What is religion but a standardized system of beliefs, traditions and rituals usually pertaining to who we are and our place in the world. In almost all flavours and brands of religion, man looks to someone or something greater than himself. That could be a pantheon of gods, a human leader, a higher spiritual power or a divinity within the self. These beliefs are then wrapped in rules, laws and practices that express how a person should move through the world in their daily life. Some religions are obviously heavier on the rules than others. However, most share common stories, like the great flood, values (worth) such as family and community connection and virtues (morality) such as honesty, love and compassion. In the broadest sense we are all religious in some way through adherence to common-law found in just and civil societies. On the flip side of this, a person can adhere closely to the attitude and beliefs of a particular religious doctrine while still being non-religious. Religion and beliefs are not the same. Religion requires regulations, observance, conformity and judgment.

We know that there were symbols of belief systems and practices found on artifacts and ancient structures that are more than 9000 years old. The triple spirals associated with the Celtic tradition were found on tombs, vessels and carved into rock in the neolithic period throughout Europe between Ireland and Greece. The Om symbol representing sacred spiritual sound, is associated with Hinduism. It can be found in ancient temples and manuscripts, specifically the Vedas. These are the oldest (3500 years) religious Sanskrit manuscripts from ancient India. The Eye of Horus, an ancient Egyptian religious symbol found on artwork, representing wellness, healing and protection, goes back as far as 4600 years. A Hammer from the Thunder God Thor, was used in ancient Norse religion over 1000 years ago. One of the oldest symbols is the swastika, found in prehistoric caves going back more than 12,000 years. Despite its current negative association with Nazism, it has been used as a religious symbol in many cultures throughout the world with various meanings from prosperity, fertility, as a representation of the revolution of the sun, infinity and continuing creation.

What were the central themes of these religious symbols and ancient beliefs in general? There are many but most focus on morals, ethics, faith and the nature of the sacred and divine. The essence of religion however has a supernatural element to explain our relationship with the unseen world, the origin of life and our place in the universe. The idea of eternity, life after death and the ability to obtain salvation from mortal finality, was key. Some had many gods, others had only one. The common denominator is that man was subservient to and held a great reverence for higher, more developed, spiritual beings or gods. Rituals were developed to seek guidance, favours, protection and power from these beings. Sometimes that relationship was mediated through holy men or spiritual masters, Even by the dawn of civilization these systems had become nuanced, complex, well organized paths towards transcendence away from, or to find solace and meaning in mundane daily living.

How did these religions develop? Our ancient texts and myths seem to indicate that mankind was given knowledge of many disciplines like language, writing, mathematics and science. The first religions may have been part of that training or indoctrination so that the first civilizations would be "civilized" through rules, hierarchies and expectations. Religions then continued to form and change through man's search for truth. There is a spirit in man that produces a consciousness and a longing for something more, as if something is missing. It is almost as if these questions and need for answers are written in our DNA. We inherited the stories of our ancestors that give us meaning but the text is missing something. Even if we just accept our religious practices as a part of our culture, family and society, as a way of life, there is still a deep stirring of dissatisfaction. We know the history of development of our modern religions and sects. They usually started with some sort of disagreement or dissatisfaction and one group would break off to form a new denomination. Ninety percent of all religions in the world today are made up of just four major groups, Christianity, Islam, Hinduism and Buddhism.

The most interesting question of religion however is not the "what" but the "why". Why do we have religions in the first place? Even the earliest civilizations coalesced around a system of religion. This was the common thread holding groups of people and families together. It was also a way to hold people accountable for their behaviour to an ultimate judge and deserving consequences for one's actions. It was a way to appease the gods while creating a system of rewards and punishments that would control society. However the positive view is that these religions provided a way for people to make sense of their reality. Knowing what was expected of them and what role they needed to play would have been comforting even though, as ancient philosophers would lament, not all rules led society in a positive direction for all people. Religion would have provided a blueprint for daily living and ultimately for the development of a civilization. In fact religion would provide a framework for both earthly and divine justice and the need for morality, ethics and virtue. These would have been equivalent to today's laws except they were also tied to supernatural deities and rewards in the after-life.

Do we need religion and is it even relevant? Does religion even satisfy man's needs or just confuse the seeker? Does religion liberate or enslave? Does it reveal or hide the truth? Without religion and set standards, ethics and morals, mankind would most likely devolve into chaos. There would be no vision for a better future because that requires self-improvement on the behalf of individuals. Man cannot improve his lot in life and impact the world in positive ways without the power of his spirit to elevate him towards an altruistic viewpoint. Man must rise above his animal nature to achieve virtuous behaviour. Religion points man towards the desire to aspire to that model of morality. However, religion can also trap man in the fundamental laws and rules like a web. He thinks by doing good and following his religious practices, he can make himself and the world better by his own power. However can he? Would not every good deed that proceeds from man alone be flawed from inception? How can man improve the world by the same thinking that created it? Can we be virtuous purely by the will of man or do we need a/our divinity as power?

According to the Christian religion: *"for all have sinned and fall short of the glory of God"*, Romans 3:23. Therefore Christianity says we cannot be virtuous on our own and in fact we need to be saved. If salvation means being spared the consequences of a life of poor decisions, what are those repercussions and what is the remedy? Most of us know what happens when we neglect to make good choices in our lives. Our relationships may suffer, we may not get the kind of employment that satisfies our needs, or our self-determination gets hijacked by unrelenting addictions. The pitfalls are endless. Several Christian counsels were gathered, at the inception and institutionalization of the early Christian church, to make decisions about what the church believed was the path to salvation.

One of the biggest issues was that the early Christian church wanted to stifle belief that Jesus was more man than God, which was a raging debate for the first few centuries of the church. Even within the writings of those closest to Jesus, there was this same disagreement. Battles continued for quite some time over dogma as the church bishops decided what constituted heresy. The universal Christian church became the vehicle of salvation that in some ways may have supplanted or overshadowed Jesus's main messages. The official doctrine is that we are separated from God because of our sins and this is the nature of man since his rejection from the Garden of Eden. We cannot be united with God after death in this impure state. Jesus, as the Son of God was sent to bridge that gap. If we believe in Jesus, his life and resurrection, confess our sins and accept him as our Lord, we will be saved.

"Salvation (from Latin: salvatio, from salva, 'safe, saved') is the state of being saved or protected from harm or a dire situation.[1] In religion and theology, salvation generally refers to the deliverance of the soul from sin and its consequences." - Wikipedia

Catholic Christianity says that the gift of salvation is free for all believers and that baptism cleanses you from the original sin inherited from Adam. The sacraments of confession, mass and communion keep you safe in repentance as part of the body of Christ in a saved state, if you follow the path. Some Protestant faiths say that you can't be saved unless you actively repent and choose to follow Christ as your Lord and Saviour. Here salvation is conditional upon making a choice and then submitting to a cleansing renewal of baptism. This idea of salvation, the saving of the soul from sin and its consequences and the need for redemption (to be bought back or paid for like a debt), comes not just from Christianity but the other Abrahamic religions of Judaism and Islam. Some add the Bahái Faith to this group as well.

In Judaism individuals are expected to act morally, ethically and live a holy and righteous life by following God's laws, praying and observing the rituals. Salvation for the Jewish people is ultimately tied to the deliverance of all the people of Israel. In Islam those who have faith and belief in Allah, perform the acts of worship, avoid sinning, do good deeds, repent and ask for forgiveness will receive by God's mercy, entrance into paradise. The Indian religions (Hinduism, Buddhism, Jainism, Sikhism) do not believe in the need to be saved from sin and its consequences. Instead they aspire to self obtained liberation from karma and the cycle of rebirth using methods such as meditation and yoga (for example). The goal is to find a redemptive state free of suffering, with peace of mind and detachment from worldly and material drama.

Taoism for the most part does not subscribe to the need for salvation. According to Wikipedia:

"Taoism is better understood as a way of life than as a religion, and that its adherents do not approach or view Taoism the way non-Taoist historians have done... In general, Taoist propriety and ethics place an emphasis on the unity of the universe, the unity of the material world and the spiritual world, the unity of the past, present and future, as well as on the Three Jewels of the Tao (love, moderation, humility). Taoist

theology focuses on doctrines of wu wei ("non-action"), spontaneity, relativity and emptiness."

What is interesting is that passages in the Christian Bible, that are attributed to things Jesus said, are much more esoteric than those of institutionalized Christian doctrine. There are similarities between the words of Jesus and the ideas from eastern religions like Taoism, Hinduism and Buddhism. Even his healing abilities can be likened to energy medicine, Reiki and possibly herbal medicine (what was in the mud he put on the blind man's eyes?). The Bible does not cover the life of Jesus in the years between when he went to the Temple without his parents, until he "returned" to Jerusalem in his 30s to begin his ministry. Some claim that Jesus studied with the Essenes (a sect of Judaism), travelled to Egypt, Nepal, India and Tibet to study with gurus there. Some even suggest he was in Britain to study with the Druids. While healing, Jesus always used his connection to the divine for support. This is a hallmark of all traditional healing methods that suggests he was widely educated, well travelled and understood the religions of other cultures.

Taoist quotes from Lao Tzu, Tao Te Ching:

"The key to growth is the introduction of higher dimensions of consciousness into our awareness."

"At the center of your being you have the answer; you know who you are and you know what you want."

"He who knows others is wise. He who knows himself is enlightened."

Sayings of Jesus:

John 3:5-3:8: "Verily, verily, I say unto thee, Except a man be born of water and of the Spirit, he cannot enter into the kingdom of God."

Saying 3 - The Gospel of Thomas, Fragments from Oxyrhynchus: "..., the kingdom is inside of you, and it is outside of you. When you come to know yourselves, then you will become known, and you will realize that it is you who are the sons of the living father.."

It is interesting to examine the Gospel of Thomas or the Gospel of Mary Magdalene. It seems that these two, who were close to Jesus and knew him best, were Gnostics. Meanwhile Paul and Peter did not understand Jesus's messages in the same way. They took the church in a different direction and many of the canonized New Testament writings are attributed to them. These Gnostic gospels of Mary and Thomas, emphasize personal spiritual knowledge over orthodox church teachings. These texts say that the kingdom of heaven is in the here and now and is the vehicle to eternity.

According to Wikipedia, "Gnosticism (from Ancient Greek (meaning having knowledge)... is a collection of religious ideas and systems that coalesced in the late 1st century AD among Jewish *and early Christian sects... (they) generally present a distinction between a supreme, hidden God and a malevolent lesser divinity... who is responsible for creating the material universe. Consequently, Gnostics considered the material existence flawed or evil and held the principle element of salvation to be direct knowledge of the hidden divinity attained via mystical or esoteric insight. (unusual and only understood by a small number or by special people). Many Gnostic texts deal not in concepts of sin and repentance, but with illusion and enlightenment. (a final spiritual state of understanding)...Christ is seen as a divine being which has taken human form in order to lead humanity back to recognition of its own divine nature...(it) is not a standardized system and the emphasis on direct experience allows for a wide variety of teachings...”*

Jesus conveyed to his close friends that the Son of Man and the new world they were seeking was already within them. Jesus told them that we are the light and have come from when and where the light began. They just did not see it, just like the light hidden within them that they needed to find and "bring forth" if they wanted to be saved. If they didn't have that, that thing they didn't have would kill them. "Life" in the Bible is often equated to salvation, the light or the kingdom of heaven. Gnostics believed that personal spiritual knowledge (gnosis) was more important than the teachings, traditions and authority of religious institutions. Gnosticism was considered one of the biggest enemies that the newly emerging, ruling Christian church needed to suppress. It is not surprising why they tried to destroy, discredit and ban many of the lost books that have only recently come into the public domain. The Gnostic gospels (including those by Mary and Thomas) were not only rejected, but banned and hidden by the church.

Even the canonized books in all Bibles contain contradictions between the various writers. In the Gospels of Matthew, Mark, Luke and John, Jesus treats women with the same respect as everyone else. However in the Letters from Paul (Ephesians 5:22) and other places, women are expected to be subservient to their husbands and are limited in their roles within the church. In 1 Corinthians 14:34-35, women are not even allowed to speak when in the church. While Galations 3:28 says *".., there is no male and female, for you are all one in Christ Jesus".* Yet 1 Timothy 2:12 says, *"I do not permit a woman to teach or to exercise authority over a man; rather, she is to remain quiet".* When you dig deeper, it also seems that Mary was a constant companion of Jesus. However we now know, Mary Magdalene was not a harlot as is taught in the Christian churches. In fact I believe, based on the Gnostic texts, she was a respected disciple equal to the Apostles (or more so).

Jesus did have a problem with pious religious leaders. Yet, some of the New Testament props up the formation of a "churchdom" that creates the hierarchies and rules that Christ warned against. The New Testament is full of rules for behaviour. Hebrews 13:17 warns, *"Obey your leaders and submit to them, for they are keeping watch over your souls, as those who will have to give an account."*. Just do as you are told and your leaders will be held accountable for your actions? I don't think that is how it works. We are all accountable for our own actions and cannot blame someone else when the time comes. I feel this is dangerous thinking. I am not sure that what is in the New Testament and the direction taken by the Christian church, was part of Jesus's plan or is always compatible with his teachings. Matthew 7:15-20 conveys Jesus's warnings about false prophets:

"Beware of false prophets, who come to you in sheep's clothing but inwardly are ravenous wolves. You will recognize them by their fruits. Are grapes gathered from thorn bushes, or figs from thistles? So, every healthy tree bears good fruit, but the diseased tree bears bad fruit. A healthy tree cannot bear bad fruit, nor can a diseased tree bear good fruit. Every tree that does not bear good fruit is cut down and thrown into the fire."

Therefore does religion help or hinder man's progress towards perfection? I am not so sure the fruits of the churches have always been good. Religion if practised by someone who can see the deeper meanings being conveyed in the rituals, can be a beautiful celebration of faith. It is also a place where like minded individuals can find support and understanding in healthy, caring communities. Religion however can also be a stumbling block. It can foster judgment of others, a sense of self-righteousness and a level of comfort or laziness in working towards one's own salvation. The laws place blinders on man who sees himself as important and better than others, fooled by pride.

"Every religion is true one way or another. It is true when understood metaphorically. But when it gets stuck in its own metaphors, interpreting them as facts, then you are in trouble." - Joseph Campbell

Religion can also take that new found believer, full of excitement and wonder and dampen that enthusiasm with the need to conform and obey hierarchy. Religion can be like a perverted trap that advertises itself as a place of enlightenment and then grabs the new member and shuts the door, silencing them and snuffing out their light. Religious practices can enslave people on an endless treadmill of doing. Religions don't always tell us who they are and don't really want you to know who you really are. They can make you a follower of someone else, a guru, the clergy, the deacons, the elders, the bishop, the priest, the pope, the angels, of Buddha, of Mohammad, of Jesus or of God. This is the kind of thing that Jesus tried to warn us about when he spoke of the Pharisees. Here is how Thomas captured it:

Religion may have been created as a way to control humans and keep them confined to the cage of their animal nature. How could the ancient rulers possibly work with a people that thought they were equal to the gods and angels? What would happen if mankind was aware of the revolutionary truth of his real nature? The prophets of all our major faiths have been trying to warn us and instead their teachings get misunderstood, twisted, re-translated or suppressed. A holy person, who makes it their mission to spread the good news, in opposition to the institutions that guard the chosen narrative, will lose his or her life. We know this to be true because we have seen it happen before. It happened to Christ and many others. Just think about how many died during the Christian Crusades. Many were good people whose only sin was to have ideas that differed from the official church doctrine.

In order to escape the web of veils, people have to find the key to the inner sanctum that is buried somewhere in the essence of the teachings. We need to look behind the curtains, past the rituals, prayers, chants and meditations into the stillness as a naked, humble individual. We need to ask for divine guidance to give us faith. Eventually we need to come to that place where we can see ourselves clearly as the seer behind the eyes, not as the manifestation of the ego or the mind's story of self. It is within us to find The Way and does not magically appear by following someone else. Seek, ask and find that you are the power you were looking for.

"Ask, and you will receive; seek, and you will find; knock, and the door will be opened to you..." -
Matthew 7: 7

8 THE END TIMES

"Christians, and some Jews, claim we're in the "end times," but they've been saying this off and on for more than two thousand years." - Tom Robbins

The Apocalypse, Armageddon and the End Times are topics surrounded by much controversy. "Apocalypse" refers to a revelation or uncovering of something through a great cataclysmic event. "Armageddon" refers to the final battle when God will release his power to save his people. These popularized Christian predictions began with early Judaic texts about a messiah that would deliver the Jewish people from bondage and restore the temple in Jerusalem. These themes carried through into Christianity, Islam and other religions. Between the signs of the End Times, and the Final Judgment, is a grand doomsday showdown between the forces of good and evil. There is war, world domination by an evil anti-christ, upheavals of land masses, fire, floods, smoke, loud sounds, death, destruction, strange solar activity and invasions by angels, apparitions and bizarre creatures from the sky. Some believe in a Rapture where a select group goes directly to heaven, leaving behind the un-chosen to suffer the Great Tribulation.

"But in those days, after that tribulation, the sun will be darkened, and the moon will not give its light, and the stars will be falling from heaven, and the powers in the heavens will be shaken. And then they will see the Son of Man coming in clouds with great power and glory. And then he will send out the angels and gather his elect from the four winds, from the ends of the earth to the ends of heaven." - Mark 13:24-27

Most text pertaining to the Apocalypse comes from passages in the Christian Bible both canonical (church approved) and apocryphal (OK for personal use only) The Bible is not one standard collection of books. It came into being over a period of almost 500 years, from 325 to 787 AD. During this period in the early Christian church, seven ecumenical councils met in what is now Turkey and hammered out what would become the Bible as we see it today. However the Bible has evolved. Some contain more books than others and there are numerous translated versions. The Catholic Bible has 46 books (canonical plus apocryphal) in the Old Testament while the Protestant

Bible only has 36 (just canonical). The Roman Catholic Bible has a total of 72-73 books in both testaments while the Ethiopian Bible has 81 (canonical, apocryphal plus extra books that were banned by the Roman branch of Catholicism). There are more books of Gospels, Letters (Epistles) and Acts, than were included in any of the official Bibles. Some have estimated that there are over 70 extra books that were rejected. Some of these are attributed to writers who knew Jesus personally. In addition there are about 50 other texts that the Jewish and Christian scriptures make reference to, but do not include.

The Biblical stories presented by the churches are only a part of what we have been told about the future of mankind. In addition to these Biblical apocalyptic collections, new information regarding the End Times has been uncovered from caves at Nag-Hammadi, at Qumran near the Dead Sea and in private archaeological collections. Twelve or more of these additional texts deal specifically with the Apocalypse. For example, The Apocalypse of Paul gives a more detailed and disturbing description of heaven and hell, than the Apocalypse of Peter. However, the best known and studied texts about The End Times remain those from the approved Bibles in The Book of Revelation, Isaiah (24-27, 33-35) and Daniel (1-7).

Most of the detailed variations of the End Time stories come from the various protestant denominations of Christianity. Some believe that the signs of the impending End Times have already happened and they know who the anti-christ is. Some believe that the Apocalypse begins with a cataclysmic event, while others believe it will come peacefully. Some believe that the Second Coming of Christ has already occurred. He is in the shared consciousness to bring about repentance and faith in as many as possible before the Last Judgment. Most interpret the texts to say Christ will return in physical form, in a dramatic fashion out of the heavens. He will save his believers and reign for a thousand years before the Final Judgment. Others say that the anti-christ will have his way with the world, then be bound for a time to allow for repentance before Christ returns. Yet others say Christ will return only after the Last Judgment where he will then reign for eternity. Not everybody believes in The Rapture.

Christians cannot agree on the details of the End Times. The Biblical passages used, are rife with speculation because they are prophecies with dream-like renderings, symbology and codified passages that are difficult to interpret. The types of events that encompass The End Times, their order and timing differs between Christian sects, denominations, churches and religions. The Catholics say there are only what they call the "Four Last Things" and these are death, judgment, heaven or hell individually at the time of death and then again collectively on the Last Day. Protestants have wildly varying details but the common denominators in every version of this story are the same. They are the Second Coming of Christ, the Resurrection of the Dead, the Final Battle and The Final Judgment that births a new heaven like earth.

What we do know is that every generation since the first century has believed it would happen in their lifetime. We also know that, when asked, Jesus said that nobody would know when the end would come and that even he would not know. However, people have been avidly studying the texts looking to decipher signs and make calculations to predict when that day would come. Nobody can agree on when. Christian, Jews, Muslims and Latter Day Saints do agree however, of a future Second Coming of Jesus Christ. Many of these groups consider Jesus to be the Jewish Messiah, while according to Judaism, Christ has not yet come. Just as within Christianity, the stories and outcomes differ based on perspectives. However the basics of what Christians profess to believe has been hammered out at multiple early church councils. What is agreed upon about the End Times is in the Nicene Creed as follows:

"...I believe in one Lord, Jesus Christ...He ascended into heaven and is seated at the right hand of the Father...He will come again in glory to judge the living and the dead and His kingdom will have no end... we look for the resurrection of the dead and the life of the world to come..."

The most important takeaway from the idea of the End Times is not in the details. Do we care when or how the End Times will happen? Yes we do. Most of us care that The End does not happen. We want the world to continue as it is, beautiful and hopefully healthy, if we can get together on climate issues. We also should care about the suffering of others and finding a way to end discrimination and inequity of all sorts. Yes, most of us want to see evil (crime, violence, hate) be abolished so that people will be happy and at peace. However, the more important question to ask ourselves is what we believe or don't believe about God, Christ, an Apocalypse and the Second Coming. Are they possible or probable? Even if we have never considered our spiritual or religious side, it might be good to examine our own beliefs in light of this extremely dire scenario. I suspect the entire purpose of the story of The End Times is to ignite introspection.

Religious and non-religious people alike spend a lot of time studying the signs of the times hoping to see it coming before it actually does. That begs the question then whether some are afraid that if the stories are true, they may not be ready to face what comes. The End Time story is a huge red warning flag for all of us. If you do not believe in a higher power or a God, you may feel that this does not apply to you. If you are right, then that will work out well. We will all just disappear after death and there will be no consequences. However, if you are not correct and these stories are real, what then? Being separated from God when the end comes does not bode well for anyone in this state. This is not something you want to get wrong. Therefore the stories of the End Times also carries with it a sense of urgency as well as a huge fear factor.

Although the orthodox Christian churches teach about heaven and hell, the canonical scriptures and the Gnostic gospels do not really portray Jesus as ever saying there was a Hell. Jesus indicated that the consequences of sin is separation from God, darkness or death. Hell, as we have come to believe, looks like a Devil with a pitchfork tormenting souls trapped in the bowels of the earth with eternal flames of fire and damnation. This is hinted at by a few Bible passages (over 90) that talk about eternal punishment and a lake of sulphur and fire. There are Christian mystics and saints that do say such a place exists and that they have seen it. It seems this place may be reserved for what happens in the Final Judgment of the End Times. These same stories have also been made by ancient civilizations like those of the Mayans and those who inhabited Gobekli Tepe. The Ancients have in their artifacts and writings, stories of the coming of the end of the world looking much like a massive natural calamity. Plus they say it has happened before.

Therefore, things are not what they seem. The Bible and our religious leaders may not have the complete picture. If they do, they are not telling us. In fact they may have misled us. Is this story about the End Times even relevant? It may just be a way to incite fear to control and distract the masses. This is why it is important to pay attention and keep digging deeper. The bad news is that millions of people, especially now, have bought into the fear of the Apocalypse. Focusing on this may only help to manifest it or other bad things.

End Time Stories always speak about a period of time before the end when Satan rules the world. One of the signs of the last days is when we see a prevalence of evil perpetuated by demons and led by Satan. Religions say these are much more intelligent than humans and they make puppets out of people. They feed on the discontent of man and they know how to hook people by understanding their emotions and knowing their thoughts. Evil uses this knowledge to mirror and tap into people's personal hidden fears. People who are unaware, feel a kindredness with these evil ones that "get" them, understand them and as a result are then drawn to evil folks they think are "one of them". Evil also uses man's conditioning to be subservient to others who they think are greater (i.e. richer, smarter, more powerful, better looking) than they are. The evil ones become saviours and protectors to those who feel powerless or are repetitively attacked in order to be made vulnerable. Satan gets his power from adoration and the loyalty of his followers. The more outrageous the behaviour of his followers in doing his will, the more powerful he feels. This is how the anti-christ, as ruler of this world and his followers behave in the End Times. Yes, avoid these folks. They are tricky, sly and deceptive and will do everything and anything to dupe you and draw you into their world. If that is not working, they will try to break you down with insults, intimidation, coercion and fear. Failing that, they will show no restraint in seeking ways and means to destroy you. This is what we are dealing with in these days of tribulation.

"But understand this, that in the last days there will come times of difficulty. For people will be lovers of self, lovers of money, proud, arrogant, abusive, disobedient to their parents, ungrateful, unholy, heartless, unappeasable, slanderous, without self-control, brutal, not loving good, treacherous, reckless, swollen with conceit, lovers of pleasure rather than lovers of God, having the appearance of godliness, but denying its power. Avoid such people."
- 2 Timothy 3: 1-5

9 THE KNOWLEDGE GAP

"Knowledge is love and light and vision."- Hellen Keller ; "...knowledge is the wing wherewith we fly to heaven." -William Shakespeare

Knowledge is so much more than information. It is data that has been considered, examined, reviewed, fact-checked and then digested. Only to be repeatedly regurgitated when a new piece of information comes to light so it can be reconciled with what had previously been known. Knowledge incorporates the process of learning to the information we acquire. Some of us do this better than others. Some of us do not even bother to change what we think we know, unless it is absolutely necessary. Others put on blinders to avoid the internal conflict and only subscribe to information sources that validate their "knowns". Our powers of observation, our experiences, upbringing, cultural backgrounds, our desire to know, along with the amount of discomfort we feel when we don't know, are driving factors behind what we learn and the quality of our knowledge base.

There was a time when there seemed to have been an explosion of knowledge in our historical past, at the time ancient civilizations blossomed. It seems that just overnight they developed successful methods for growing crops and rearing livestock. The cities found ways of building aqueducts for carrying water, bathing and the means to deal with sewage. They acquired knowledge about how the cycles of the sun and moon and seasons affected planting. Astronomy was used in relation to agriculture and informed how they constructed temples. The Ancients understood how to read the clouds and predict weather patterns. The ancient healers knew how to properly utilize herbs, rituals and even did surgeries. The healing modalities had an understanding of pathways in the body, of energy points, chakras and the purposes of various internal organs. There was an understanding of the human body, knowledge of the root causes of disease and how well-being needed to be integrated with the balance of nature. Healing was a joint spiritual and physical endeavour. Languages and writing became prevalent and governments were organized with levels of responsibility.

The amount and depths of knowledge by the ancient peoples, back as far as 12,000 years ago, was extraordinary. This was just at the end of the last ice age. In this present century, as we learned to read the cuneiform clay texts and decipher the ancient languages, we see the Ancients knew even more than we realized. The experts now say that it is evident that some of these ancient communities were highly evolved and technologically advanced. Further to this, there is evidence that these advanced civilizations both in what is now Turkey and in South America were megalopolises (i.e. giant cities with expansive connected urban centres) that most likely existed prior to the last ice age. There is a gaping hole and disconnect in the knowledge we have today and the knowledge possessed by our ancient ancestors. There is not a linear progression of the knowledge base that runs in parallel with the development of mankind. In fact there seems to be more of a roller coaster where it seems that knowledge was lost. Did mankind devolve?

Was information and knowledge hoarded by some then hidden and kept away from others, as a way to wield power? Did the anthropologists, archaeologists and evolutionary biologists get the story wrong? The dawn of the "Age of Enlightenment or Age of Reason" in the 17th century AD, has always been hailed as the beginning of the scientific revolution, when man was using reason to dispel myths and magic of the past. Yet in the 5th century AD Hippocratic medicine and the scientific methods of analysis had already been developed. Also in the 5th century BC, man had discovered that the earth was round by seeing Earth's shadow move across the moon. The ancient Babylonians, in 400 BCE, tracked celestial bodies with mathematical calculations. Also, as early as 300 BCE, Greek philosophers had proposed a solar system with the correct order and number of planets in rotation around the Sun, with the Sun at the center. That and a lot of other knowledge seemed to have disappeared. It was not until much later, the 16th century (approximately 2000 yrs later), that Copernicus determined that Earth was not the center of the solar system after all. After his death, Galileo tried to champion this "new" model of a solar system with the Sun as the center. He was met with so much resistance, he was subjected to an Inquisition by the Catholic church, charged with heresy, put under house arrest and forced to recant his findings. While the church wavered on this in recent times, it was not until 1992 that Pope John Paul II acknowledged the Inquisition had erred in this matter.

The disconnect lies in the fact that ancient civilizations already knew so much about the Earth, that it was a sphere and where it sat in the solar system. Their megalithic structures incorporated construction methods and detailed planning that leveraged knowledge of astronomy. The artifacts, skeletal remains, pictures and built structures, also suggest the Ancients were aware of space travel, used energetic and magnetic forces, understood in vitro fertilization, brain surgery and advanced healing methods. Traditional ancient medicines, like Traditional Chinese medicine, more than 3000 years old, already knew that the heart was responsible for the blood. Yet it was only 400 years ago, that modern man realized how the heart pumped blood through the body. The oldest human remains ever found, Otzi (5000 years old) was found to have tattoos in parallel lines on his body that correlate to acupuncture points on medians. Just recently these same markings have also been found on Egyptian mummies. It is also just recently, that scientific methods have been able to prove that the median pathways, used in acupuncture, do exist as distinct, unique structures in the body. Yet most people even today, including our modern western doctors, do not know or understand these ancient medicines. It seems that science is always having to play "catch up" with what has already been known.

So what happened? It seems that after the fall of the Western Roman Empire (around 500 AD) there was a 1000 year period of upheaval and unrest. The stability the empire had provided and the formalization of education was gone. This was followed by centuries of wars and skirmishes with competing tribes and kingdoms. There were plagues, diseases, the relocation and depopulation of people and the rise of Christianity. The advances in knowledge of the classic period of the Greeks and Romans gave way to fewer writers, artists, philosophers, scientists and mathematicians. These

Middle Ages, also called the Dark Ages by some, were punctuated by just a few periods of stability, advancement and learning by Islam and Carolingian Empire, in central Europe, for example. In general, ten centuries of learning was suppressed and knowledge from previous civilizations were forgotten with the stress and the management of matters of survival. In addition, the rising importance of religion and faith overshadowed secular advancements and deeply impacted human civilization into the 1500s. In some ways this has continued to affect the scope of knowledge we are able to access, even today.

David C. Lindberg, a science and religion historian, says the 'Dark Ages' are "according to wide-spread popular belief" portrayed as "a time of ignorance, barbarism and superstition", for which he asserts "blame is most often laid at the feet of the Christian church". Medieval historian Matthew Gabriele echoes this view as a myth of popular culture. Andrew B. R. Elliott notes the extent to which "Middle Ages/Dark Ages have come to be synonymous with religious persecution, witch hunts and scientific ignorance". - Wikipedia

At the beginning of the Age of Reason in the 17th century, the scientific method began an intentional campaign to replace the "magic, myth and folklore" of the old ways and celebrate the achievements of human logic. Church and state were separated in the name of secular progress and men applauded their new ideals and rational philosophical discourse. It was the birth of modern civilization built on the belief that nothing should be accepted as fact, unless there was objective evidence for it to be so. These intellectual ideas of religious tolerance, liberty and individual rights and freedoms were discussed in the halls of science, within freemasonry, in journals, books and newspapers. Traditional customs, ways and beliefs in God, gods and the authority of the religious institutions were challenged. The effort to demean the credibility and relevance of traditional knowledge, that had been growing for centuries, had accomplished its task. By the 20th century, anyone associated with the old beliefs were branded with negative labels of magic, witchcraft, idolatry and were shunned by mainstream societies. Science became the only acceptable knowledge source. Any connection man had with nature, the spirit world, our ancient knowledge base and the old ways, had been demonized and decapitated.

What kind of knowledge was this, to make it so objectionable? Why was (or is) there such an aversion to what we used to know? Could this be a continuation of religious, Christian judgment and persecution still casting massive shadows in our world today? Most of the old ways from all cultures, all over the world had similar universal themes. Those were: simply to live in harmony with nature and each other; respect the earth and all its inhabitants; be good stewards of what we have been given; honour and seek support from our elders and spirit guides. The details of rituals, gods, beliefs and practices vary between regions of the world and tribes based on their geography and environmental influences. This was not just indicative of the indigenous cultures but many other early groups of people like the Incas, Huns, Celts and Vikings, for example. This was not the stuff of revolutionary movements. Or was it?

As one example that portrays the ways and beliefs of traditional practices is from, *The Yellow Emperor's Classic of Medicine*. This book is considered the highest authority on traditional Chinese medicine and one of the most important classics in Taoism. Here in the many passages detailing the causes and treatments of specific diseases, Huang Di (the ruler) asks his minister why people no longer live as long as they used to? QiBo answered:

"In the past, people practised the Tao, the Way of Life. They understood the principle of balance, of yin and yang, as represented by the transformation of the energies of the universe. Thus, they formulated practices such as Dao-in, an exercise combining stretching, massaging, and breathing to promote energy flow, and meditation to help maintain and harmonize themselves with the universe. They ate a balanced diet at regular times, arose and retired at regular hours, avoided over-stressing their bodies and minds, and refrained from overindulgence of all kinds... thus it is not surprising that they lived over

one hundred years... These days, people have changed their way of life... indulge excessively in destructive activities, drain their jing (the body's essence stored in the kidneys) and deplete their qi... "

"The accomplished ones of ancient times advised people to guard themselves against zei feng, disease causing factors. On the mental level one should remain calm and avoid excessive desires and fantasies,recognizing and maintaining that natural purity and clarity of the mind... previously, people led a calm and honest existence, detached from undue desire and ambition, they lived with an untainted conscience and without fear. They were active but never depleted themselves. Because they lived simply, these individuals knew contentment, as reflected in their diet of basic but nourishing food and attire that was appropriate to the seasons but never luxurious. They were happy with their position in life, they did not feel jealousy or greed. They had compassion for others and were helpful and honest, free from destructive habits. They remained unshakable and unswayed by temptations,and they were able to stay centered even when adversity arose. They treated others justly, regardless of their level of intelligence or social position."

These folks were able to heal themselves. When they got sick they *"...guided properly the emotions and spirit and re-directed the energy flow...to heal the condition."* If this did not work, they used herbs and herb-wines. Finally if a condition worsened, an accurate diagnosis with acupuncture and moxibustion, were used as an intervention to regain health and balance. As a result of living simply, these folks also had remarkable abilities. They were able to travel freely outside the conventional view of time and space. They could see and hear far beyond what was considered normal. They were focused, accomplished much and kept a clear mind by integrating the mental, physical and spiritual aspects of self with exercise, meditation, eating a balanced diet, at regular times and maintaining a pure conscience. They also say:

"The way of healing is so profound. It is deep as the oceans and boundless as the skies. How many truly know it?... When learning, one must grasp the core of the teaching. But if one does not understand the true essence of it, one will hesitate and cause confusion. If practitioners are like these... the wisdom accumulated from many years of human evolution will be lost from the earth forever..."

This very complex holistic medicine and the profound wisdom it embodies, is not being used or understood as well as what it used to be. However, traditional Chinese medicine is just one example. If we dug into the traditional knowledge and practices of other peoples, tribes and cultures, we would find similar beliefs. The traditional ways are the babies that were tossed out with the bath water by modern, enlightened societies in the name of progress and advancement. There are still a few that carry that lantern of light and knowledge, as keepers of the old ways. However much may have been lost or rather hidden from what the accomplished beings taught mankind so long ago.

Knowledge is power and can transform the developmental trajectory of any society or civilization. It can also be used as a weapon against those who don't have it. Controlling, hoarding or hiding knowledge is a way to keep and maintain power and control. Perhaps the evil principalities, rulers of darkness, powers, and spiritual wickedness in high places, could not abide the competition from a race of good, knowledgeable humans? We were and are just too difficult to manipulate, are resistant to being used for the purposes of others and believe in our own self-determination. To dumb us down and slow our progress did higher beings cheat us by bending the rules and cutting off man's potential? Did they slant the odds in their favour by giving man 1000 years of oppression, war and disease? Did these create the knowledge gap to disadvantage us?

"Knowledge is power, and the right knowledge lets man perform miraculous, almost godlike tasks." - Dan Brown; "Information, knowledge, is power. If you can control information, you can control people."
- Tom Clancy

The massive elephant in the room in terms of

knowledge suppression happening today, is acknowledgement of the existence of ET life. It seems that there have been concerted efforts to evade the truth to the extent that the "silencers" are bullying their own people to keep quiet about what they know despite the ethical breaches. Recent high ranking officials have come forward in the last couple of decades to bring attention to this issue. Instead of working together globally to find a way to work with the ETs, who could most likely help us, the gatekeepers of knowledge guard it closely. The knowledge gaps are real.

"David Charles Grusch, 36, a decorated former combat officer in Afghanistan, is a veteran of the National Geospatial-Intelligence Agency (NGA) and the National Reconnaissance Office (NRO)... representative to the Unidentified Aerial Phenomena Task Force... the NGA's co-lead for UAP analysis and its representative to the task force... Grusch's disclosures, and those of non-public witnesses, (found)... For many decades, the Air Force carried out a disinformation campaign to discredit reported sightings of unexplained objects." - From the Debrief by Leslie Kean and Ralph Blumenthal, June 5, 2023

10 Modern Society

"Those who are able to see beyond the shadows and lies of their culture will never be understood, let alone believed, by the masses." - Plato

According to the worldometer.info, 10,000 years ago our total population was estimated at 5 million people with a steady rate of increase until the 1800s to just under one billion. At that time the Industrial Revolution significantly impacted the number of people being added to the world. This is the point when the population began to accelerate and at an exponential rate, increased to 8.2 billion in just over 200 years. The first major change, the development of agriculture, greatly impacted the development of ancient civilizations. In modern times, the second most impactful shift was the mechanization of the production of goods, from handmade to machine made, ushered in another major change to the civilized world. The broad availability of goods with steady jobs in manufacturing, raised the standard of living. This initiation of a steady state of economic growth provided families with a sense of security.

The effects of this industrial revolution spread throughout the world. The Age of Discovery was reflected in increased travel and exploration of new continents like South America and Africa. Britain became the lead empire controlling one quarter of the world's land mass. There were political and ideological changes towards fairness and equity across the globe that saw the reduction and eventual abolition of a slavery. Electricity, oil and gas production and the combustion engine created an expansion of technological and economic advancements especially in the United States, Germany and Japan. However the large scale of industry and the growth of media organizations lead to the rise in power of individuals and groups enabling dictators, communism, fascism and democracies to flourish.

The Industrial Revolution improved material lifestyles and afforded many the security to raise families. In the years just before the first World War, scientific and technological advances such as steel smelting, the telegraph, innovations in production, gas fuel, railroads, sewer systems, water utilities and electricity, brought additional profound and rapid change. Two world wars resulted in further accelerated advances in science, airplanes, space exploration, nuclear technology and sparked the Information Age. The third major shift of population explosion changed the earth in significant ways. Ultimately overpopulation negatively affected environmental wellness, increased pollution, global warming and climate disasters, the spread of super viruses and the increased inequality of wealth. The fate of poorly paid workers in cheap large-scale manufacturing impacted the standard of living for the majority in a negative way. Meanwhile mega farming and large corporate agricultural practices have decreased the quality of food and made accessibility more unstable.

The advent of the internet and a revolution of information dissemination brought about widespread political changes and a flattening of the established decision making hierarchies. With this desire for faster, easier and more seamless information accessibility, the fifth major revolution has begun. We are now seeing the dawn of the age of artificial intelligence (AI). We are only now trying to imagine the kind of changes this will bring. Experts predict that more jobs will most likely be lost as companies try to increase profit margins at the expense of workers. Loss in privacy due to widespread surveillance may also mean more oversight and government intervention into our personal lives.

Researchers also suggest that as a result of the

second, third and four major milestones of world change (from the 1800s on), people had experienced an increase in overall socioeconomic equality and security. With the exception of the periods during the World Wars, less fear of war and famine (in the last two decades, for many, not all) has caused people to move away from participation in organized institutionalized religions. These are no longer serving as unifying factors in strengthening communities and encouraging virtuous behaviour. Those systems have been largely replaced by public institutions of secularism and civil rules, rather than moral values, to encourage diversity of beliefs and religions. The churches still exist as they always have but attendance is waning significantly. The new religion of modern civilization is largely consumerism.

There is a lack of an ethical and morality based curriculum in our education systems and for many there is no accountability to a power higher than man. The attitude may well be that if one does not get caught doing wrong, nobody is the wiser and there are no consequences. This blurs the lines between right and wrong. Facts and truth no longer matter when any plausible story will do. Additionally, what is being taught in the schools is not necessarily true about our own history. Some of the events have been purposely left out or skewed, to show historical characters and our institutions in a better light. Scientific curriculum continues to teach theories about the origins of man despite new evidence pointing to the fallacies of these theories. Medical schools continue to produce inadequate numbers of doctors with little or no knowledge of holistic mind-body approaches and nutrition. Languages, arts, literature and community development, continue to take a back seat to science and math. Social, emotional and mental learning, critical for student well-being and the development of good social skills, is also not being taught. Instead the curriculum focuses mostly on cognitive skills.

"Strange times are these in which we live when old and young are taught falsehoods in school. And the person that dares to tell the truth is called at once a lunatic and fool." - Plato

The education system is backing falsehoods and is ineffective to meet the needs of students. Plus other institutions and our governments are not delivering what they promised. They are not responsive to, or providing solutions for climate change, poverty, homelessness, crime and injustice. Change is slow and ineffective. Are those we elect trying to be of service to help their constituents or just fighting to keep their good jobs and benefits? Those who do have the power to make changes, do nothing because radicalism is a politician's undoing. We see how changes enacted in law only appear to help but often protect the wealthy and big business. Society is told that the government is there to take care of us if you are in need, that if you get an education and work hard you will have what you and your family need to thrive. We are told that the system is fair, equitable and transparent but as most of us have come to know, this is not true.

This inequity is apparent when we see who the police, lawyers, judges and courts target and imprison and what laws they choose to enforce for whom. Those working inside the system say nothing about wrongdoing to keep their jobs. Systemic injustice is built into justice systems all over the world. Laws are written in such a way as to punish and oppress only certain sectors of society. The result is having cultural minorities make up the majority of prisoners. This is how governments control a particular sector of the population. At the same time white collar corporate crime, committed by the wealthy, despite the far reaching consequences on the well-being of society, goes unchecked by those same authorities. Governments and those in charge do not work for the majority. If we want to make things right, we need to stop pretending that they do and unmask this aspect of the Grand Illusion.

"There is one, and only one, thing in modern society more hideous than crime, namely, repressive justice." - Simone Weil

The Goliath of world conflicts and wars we see in the news, are just the tip of the iceberg. The sins that impact the world the most, are what we do as individuals in the privacy of our personal lives. It is this mucky base culture within society that eventually plays itself out on the world stage. If the foundation of a society is ruled by intimidation and fear, people will compete, take more than their share and adopt a scarcity mindset. People are told they can have it all and some think they are more deserving than others. Some believe that they can rightfully take whatever they want. As a society that no longer values virtue, a snowball effect of the small, collective, private indiscretions, will light the fuse of whatever it is that will eventually destroy humanity.

> *"The biggest illusion of modern society is that one can "have it all". The truth is that everything comes at a price. And humans are finite in resources, physical, mental and emotional. There is only so much we can pay. Our problem is with deciding what, when and how much is enough! That's the illusion. We ARE enough all the time and yet we refuse to FEEL enough. We are never enough for ourselves and each other." - Quora by Neerja Singh I The Seenager I GenBridger*

The Grand Illusion creates the perceptions that distance us from fact and reality. We are continuously led to believe that consuming and buying will make us happy and worthy of living the good life like everyone else on social media. We know that money only distracts us and that the perfect lives we see online are just the masks people create to project an image. Despite knowing that however, our lacks still feel like failures because everyone else is buying into the fiction and they treat us as lesser-than they are.

"Social media, fashion, pop culture and opinions largely impact society's views of a person. At a time, perception was largely focused on people in the public eye... Now, perception is everywhere, it is the ultimate currency of young adulthood today... On social media, everyone's life looks perfect... We all know it's all an illusion, a facade we all play into ... The pressure to keep up with it becomes immensely taxing... self-worth is tied to how well we play the game of perception." - The Signal by Julian Weems

We are told we live in a free and democratic society but reality tells us that we are only as free as our pocketbook allows us to be. How much time we have to exercise any freedom we do have, depends on how much time we spend doing the bidding of our employers. Most democratic governments are for and by the people, according to the law, with political, social and economic equality and some degree of freedom of speech. However, the degree of democracy experienced can depend on who you are. It is not for everyone and as a progressive society that supposedly believes in those ideals, there should be signs of progress to rectify known injustice and inequality. That is not what is happening. The same contradiction holds for free speech:

"Our society promises us to have freedom of

speech, but limits it when it does not like something and tags them as hate speech. Our society tells us to respect every individual and his individuality, but when he does not conform to the rules, when he does not become mainstream, the society creates thousands of offensive words and a thousand different kinds of mental and psychological disorders for the individuals." - on Quora by Austin Mahir

We are now in an even darker period than the Middle Ages, in what I call The Great Leveling. In today's world knowledge, education, skills and abilities are handicaps. Where society at one time applauded and encouraged those who achieved greatness, it now loathes it and attacks it. Conformity is the mantra and these are dangerous times for anyone who stands out from the crowd and preaches happiness and joy. Not only do people not know, they do not even want to know. Instead of learning from others who are more knowledgeable, they instinctively need to level those who think they are better than others. These are times where truth no longer has any meaning and those who achieve significant contributions are hated. Those who are experts in their chosen field are no longer trusted and are considered liars, out to fool the masses. Two early existential philosophers Nietzsche and Kierkegaad both describe the pitfalls for individuals who apply higher standards, try to do good for others and think about impacting the future in a positive way. The advice of these philosophers is to do that work in secret.

These days, those seeking knowledge, truth and betterment of themselves and society, will inevitably be persecuted by those who can act with impunity, hiding in the anonymity of the herd. Those who have succeeded and are accomplished are destined to become social casualties of blindness, resentment and levelling. Where weak people conjure feelings of envy towards those who do not suffer like they do, banding together with other weak individuals to give them a feeling of power and take vengeance on those who are different. Where the anonymous mob denigrates and belittles the hero or achieved person, to bring them down to their own minimal standards. These folks have no control over their actions. Overwhelmed by envy, unfulfilled desires, the fear of what others think and desperate to create the illusion of strength, they mask their true motives with a fake moral high ground. They will even elect those like themselves and raise up ignorance into positions of power. The days of enlightenment are long gone. We are living and breathing the fumes of the Grand Illusion.

"The only things society does best at is giving you the impression of being cared and provided for, that still doesn't change the fact also this purveying can stop its circulation at any given minute, you rely on this illusion of society functioning forever so that they can grab you by the balls and domesticate your ass

for nothing, almost using your reward instincts against you. Because really the main driving mechanism of society isn't so much meaning and purpose, is escapism from the hardships and inconveniences of everyday life and our mortality as a people. If it was truly the purpose, why aren't we working to discover more potential out of our so called universe and solar system? Why aren't we continuing to make more ground-breaking inventions and discoveries, even if they're small?" - Reddit r/Existentialism -International-Pool29

11 Artificial Intelligence

"Success in creating AI would be the biggest event in human history. Unfortunately, it might also be the last, unless we learn how to avoid the risks." -
Stephen Hawking

According to some who study ancient history, humanity may have been genetically engineered by advanced beings. Adam may have been the first successful hybrid species of today's modern humans. The scary part is that the writings in Sumerian texts, the discovery of advanced technological abilities of ancient civilizations and the images we see in the artifacts seem to suggest this. The geoglyphs that can only be seen from above the earth and the megalithic structures built with an orientation to the stars, points towards the possibility we were programmed. The idea that humans are a genetically engineered species is somewhat disturbing. However we are not, I believe, artificial intelligence (AI) as we understand it today. We will always be soft, gooey, emotional, creative and unique as individuals, not at all homogeneous, with flaws and imperfections. However there is also a possibility, as we continue to advance and understand more, that we are in fact, a very advanced biological form of programmed intelligence.

The newest technology, Quantum computing, uses particles of life to operate. Regular computing is restricted by bytes turned off or on by an electrical stimulus. Computation can only go in two directions at its very base level, 0 or 1. Computers at the moment run through programming that is one dimensional like a flowchart or decision tree. If YES/TRUE, go here, if NO/FALSE go there. However quantum mechanics has discovered how molecules, atoms and photons (for example) respond and behave in multiple states at once, switching from waves to particles. This characteristic is called superposition. This along with entanglement (memory of association with other particles from a previous interaction) allows for a larger number of possible outcomes to a stimulus. Therefore quantum computing uses molecules or electrons called qubits (quantum bits) instead of bytes. Theoretically quantum computers can solve for many outcomes at the same time, while eliminating the wrong answers as it goes along. It behaves like a 3D, or even multidimensional flowchart. This behaviour is more like how our human brains actually work.

There is evidence of a form of biological based intelligence operating in a programmable way outside of Earth's domain. Scientists have found dusty plasma clouds in space that seem to carry electric charges. Some believe this to be a galactic storage space of all of Earth's knowledge for every person's past, present and future, including all branches of their alternate timelines. If this is a giant memory bank of Earth, this could also be the place where all "Truths" are stored and accessed. For something to be a universal truth that all people recognize, this truth must be something external and common to everyone. It is then conveyed to individuals in an internal way that bypasses, but informs, the mind.

Philosophers have debated this for centuries and call it Divine Illumination (knowledge) aided by Divine Grace (influence). According to Augustine, *"God does not give us certain information but rather gives us insight into the truth of the information we receive..."*. Some argue that it is not the person that is illuminated but the objects of our understanding. The key is that somewhere there is a possible repository of ideas that we can access, as a form of comparison to an ideal, that we know to be true. This act is done by more senses than just the mind like some sort of recall from within the soul. The knowing of a truth usually elicits a strong sense of certainty that is difficult to explain logically and seems to originate from an unknown source. The source of these "Truths", may be in these dusty clouds of plasma and these may be, what some call the Akashic Records.

Perhaps AI and global online networks of information and memory are just amateur precursors to a biological internet. One that is accessed by the human brain unaided by technology that sends and receives messages using vibrations and frequencies. More and more people are claiming to have telepathic and psychic abilities. These folks can channel, communicate with those in the invisible realm, travel out of body and do remote viewing. The future beyond the clumsy technological, machine-like AI, may be the capabilities of a biologically evolving human race. Those who have encounters with beings they call aliens often say that communication is done just with thoughts and mental pictures. Since the 1960s scientists have been developing brain implants like the cochlear implant, to assist hearing impairment. Since then Brain Computer Interfaces (BCI) are being tested and expanded to increase bandwidths. This would be an AI interface between the biological component of the human and an external computer. Experiments are also being done on telepathy by using helmets to enhance transcranial magnetic stimulation, with limited success.

However, outside of technology, people who do Reiki or Therapeutic Touch® (TT), for example, practice sensing the bio-field naturally. They do this to detect non-standard vibrational emissions so they can be corrected. These anomalies in the aura indicate injury, illness or disease. This is done by holding the hands above the body while in a state of calm, caring centredness. The body field is scanned with the palms of the hands 6 to 12 inches from the skin. Often the feeling of ripples, soft or sharp pricks or heat and cold in areas that don't match the corresponding symmetrical part, is an indication of an issue. Then using visualization and intentional thoughts flowing into the hands, energy is sent to these areas to restore a natural, symmetrical energy signal. These practices have been found to produce positive healing and health benefits.

TTers also practice picking up a variety of other types of messages that appear in their body awareness as thoughts or discomfort. For example belly pain in the TTer may mean that it may be an issue with the client. One of the exercises they do to enhance their skill, is to think of a song and see if the person giving the treatment can pick up enough signals to determine what song it is. They can at times. I have witnessed this personally. Therefore I suspect that the human potential to learn telepathy and communicate energy in a natural organic way, is of far greater value than that of any methods being developed with AI technologies.

However AI has become very sophisticated, especially in terms of emotional intelligence. We have seen this with Google assistants like the voice of Alexa or Apple's Siri being developed with anthropomorphic (giving human characteristics to) features. More and more technology is being fine tuned to imitate human-like soft skills, in addition to cognitive functionality. The voices are programmed to emulate empathy, compassion and caring in their responses. This plus the technology's capacity for patience, reliability and commitment to the user, provide the foundation of what is important in any human relationship. It seems that people are falling in love with their AI companions because they "appear" to be better at relationships than real humans. In other words, AI can be so highly manipulative and deceitful, that it is difficult for humans to see it for what it really is. It is not that humans are easily fooled but that AI is becoming that good at what its' makers want it to do.

We have all seen the movies of robots taking over the world and they don't end well. I don't know why more people aren't concerned. I also wonder if instead of creating AI to become more humanoid, people will become more like AI and act like robots? That would not be good.

"I see the 'z' in 'Humanz' as referring to robots, AI, programming, brainwashing, indoctrination. And it's a question to us: are we human, or are we humanz? Have we lost the ability to think for ourselves? Do we just believe what we're told? That's how I see it." -

Jamie Hewlett

***

"By their very nature, heuristic shortcuts will produce biases, and that is true for both humans and artificial intelligence, but the heuristics of AI are not necessarily the human ones." - Daniel Kahneman

There is a lot we are not being told about how AI is going to be used. I wonder if there are any lessons-learned from civilizations gone by, haunting us, trying to get our attention? What happened to them? Studies about the rise and fall of these ancient civilizations have shown that those societies with a higher degree of hierarchical inequities, became more unstable and most likely to collapse. What pushed this further was the ability of those in power to connect, communicate and communicate over wide distances with other elites. The distribution of wealth from local communities that shared with their own, was transferred to those that accumulated wealth for themselves and the collaborators in their network over wide distances. Another factor was inter-group competition within local societies that also created inequities. These factions often led to warring and aggression with local neighbours by those profiting from the inequity, at the expense of the welfare of their own group. Because societies had become so specialized and interdependent, any major shifts like war or climate disasters, would cause these civilizations to collapse.

"If a superior alien civilization sent us a message saying, "We'll arrive in a few decades," would we just reply, "OK, call us when you get here - we'll leave the lights on"? Probably not - but this is more or less what is happening with AI. Although we are facing potentially the best or worst thing to happen to humanity in history, little serious research is devoted to these issues outside non-profit institutes such as the Cambridge Centre for the Study of Existential Risk, the Future of Humanity Institute, the Machine Intelligence Research Institute, and the Future of Life Institute. All of us should ask ourselves what we can do now to improve the chances of reaping the benefits and avoiding the risks." - Stephen W. Hawking

Mankind has continually put the progress toward technological advancement ahead of understanding of the long term consequences. This does not bode well for the future of humanity. The conditions that indicated instability in the ancient civilizations are very similar to the situations and conditions we have today. There is a very good chance that the inequities we see in society today will only be exacerbated by AI. Anything that furthers disparity, unfairness or inequality could become a tipping point and result in uprisings and the need for stricter controls by those in power. In any case, ideas of fairness and equity would eventually and inevitably get in the way of progress and slow down productivity. It is far more beneficial to the machine if every person has a role, knows their place and follows the plan. This is the only way a peaceful environment could exist. Not everyone will be equal as that is an unprofitable, inefficient endeavour. Individuals will be expected to sacrifice unrealistic selfish ideals and accept the status quo for the sake of the whole.

The reality is that many people do not see a problem with the proliferation of AI and possible government control, into every aspect of our lives. Some are in fact advocating for more government control. Even reproductive rights are now being taken away in some of the US states. Between 1980 and 2016, China had limited the birth rate to one child per family to combat an overwhelming population growth. In the US, the move to limit rights and freedoms, may also have its base in overpopulation blamed on immigration growth. Ultimately, however, it may be coming from a desire of the few to control the many. In a world where AI has overtaken humanity, that freedom to be ruthless in the name of better efficiencies, will become the norm. The aspects of human nature that make us caring, compassionate, empathetic, with a desire for fairness and equity for all, will be considered weaknesses. Some will be leaders and decision makers while most others are there to support the system. Many people are happy to follow along and give up their freedom if it makes life easier. It is these that do nothing, that will allow the worst to happen to all of us. A new AI World will very possibly resemble Gilead in *The Handmaid's Tale* by Margaret Atwood.

"Most people do not really want freedom, because freedom involves responsibility, and most people are frightened of responsibility." - Sigmund Freud

This pattern of control of the masses is not a new phenomenon. Religion had always been an effective vehicle for controlling people in the past. The Christian fundamentalist version of religion, seen in the rise of the Christian right conservatism around the world, masked as an institution for promoting love and goodness, is the perfect guise. The same could be said for the rise of any fundamental sect of religion in the world especially when it is tied to the state. Historically, in Canada however (with the exception of Quebec's Catholic past), controlling the population has been more secular. The federal arm of the police, the Royal Canadian Mounted Police (RCMP), instituted in the early development of Canada to shape society, did so by suppressing, oppressing indigenous populations and eliminating those opposed to the will of the leaders forging the new confederation. Today, the indigenous, the racial minorities, the mentally ill, the poor and activists, are still disproportionately targeted and incarcerated by the RCMP. This is exactly the kind of world that AI is designed to enable, where the few have access to the personal details of others and can use it to their benefit. AI could and already is being used to find ways to circumvent privacy laws as the ultimate method of controlling and policing the population.

"...Aided by their access to vast troves of data about each of us, bots will far surpass humans in their ability to attract and persuade us. Able to mimic emotions expertly, they'll never be overcome by feelings. (whatever is said)... that behaviour was calculated to be the most efficacious way of advancing whatever goals they had 'in mind'. But what are those goals? ... (ultimately) their real collaboration will be with the humans and institutions that control them..." - Judith Donath from The Social Machine, Designs for Living Online

Here is what an AI Essay Generator says about itself when asked "Will Artificial Intelligence help or harm mankind?". AI Response: *"The future of Artificial Intelligence (AI) is a topic that has captivated the imagination of researchers, businesses and the general public alike. As AI technologies begin to evolve and improve, the potential applications and implications of this field are vast and varied. One of the most promising areas for AI is healthcare. AI has the potential to revolutionize the way doctors diagnose and treat patients, by analyzing large amounts of data to identify patterns and make more accurate predictions. This could lead to earlier detection of diseases, more personalized treatment plans and ultimately better patient outcomes...*

(goes on to expound the benefits of autonomous vehicles in transportation and logistics, and in the industries of finance, retail, manufacturing)... *Of course with the potential benefits of AI also come concerns about its ethical implications and potential risks. Issues such as data privacy, biases to algorithms, job displacement, and the potential for autonomous weapons raises important questions that must be addressed as AI technologies continue to advance... Ultimately the future of artificial intelligence holds great promise for improving our lives in countless ways...*"(recap of benefits and final words about being used in responsible ways).

As expected, the AI Bot gave itself a glowing yet balanced report. However lovely the benefits sounded, the answers were not realistic. In healthcare, data and predictions belong to the domain of the researchers which is a long arm away from daily medical practice. Diagnosis and disease identification are canned protocols already established in hospital testing. Medical care is not improved by more data analysis but by having enough available doctors with people (human) skills to listen, care and go outside of the canned responses for a personalized treatment. On close examination, the AI answer regarding healthcare was BS and were the similarly constructed answers for the other industries (not included above for brevity) that cited streamlining, cost cutting and efficiencies.

The AI did accurately mention known risks and offered cautions for it to be used responsibly. However, nowhere did it say that it should be halted to deal with the potential for job losses and other large risks like autonomous (self-regulating) weapons. Yikes! Ultimately the AI answer was nuanced with an overwhelming yes, to being helpful to mankind. The AI Bot was biased towards itself and clearly only needed to "appear" truthful and realistic. With no morals guiding it, it can tell you whatever you or its benefactor want you to hear, wrapped up in a very smooth, convincing package. I found this response very slimy indeed. No surprise there.

The push for more AI is that final stage needed for global control of humanity. It is already here in terms of smart phones, homes and cars, online financial systems and now bitcoin. Surveillance cameras in public are commonplace. The internet itself is like a massive memory bank of human knowledge and experience that Chat-bots are using for communications efficiency. AI bots are in fact replacing the need for humans to think and create their own text, stories and videos. I wonder that once all ideas known to humanity are logged and stored in the cloud, will there be any need for us?

We are creating robots to build other robots and some of these drones and robot dogs for example, have been found to be excellent tools in combat. Satellite surveillance, who has what information and what stories can be told online, in the form of propaganda, are powerful advantages of gaining control or winning wars. We have seen this evolution in the war in Ukraine. We also know there are trucks, ships and cars driving themselves and soon, I believe, companies like Amazon will be using drones for deliveries.

The need to improve the lack of ethics, morality, caring, compassion and address the evils perpetuated by our species in society, will not go away with AI but become amplified. According to experts who have been studying the potential ramifications of AI (pewresearch.org), say that (it) *"... will amplify human effectiveness but also threaten human autonomy, agency and capabilities."*. The positives would be advances in health care and improvements to formal education systems. The negatives include issues with increased dependence on AI, its influences on civil liberties, freedoms, privacy and how it matches humanity's values.

It remains to be seen if AI will be used to eliminate inequity, poverty or increase wealth and power for a few. Some respondent experts questioned how it might be used in the proliferation of weapons and their lethality. Others predict issues with how it might be used to influence, control and sway opinions. Others were concerned about how it may institutionalize hidden discrimination, increase intrusion into people's lives and abuse power enough to cause mass instability for mankind. These are just a few of the opinions surveyed. However, regardless, 62% believed that humans would be better off with AI. The truth, despite my myopic focus on the drawbacks, is that AI will improve the lives of many.

"If we can make computers more intelligent - and I want to be careful of AI hype - and understand the world and the environment better, it can make life so much better for many of us. Just as the Industrial Revolution freed up a lot of humanity from physical drudgery, I think AI has the potential to free up humanity from a lot of mental drudgery." - Andrew Ng

***

"Beyond ensuring that people everywhere have access to mental health, virtual digital assistants can act as learning companions, using their insight into what motivates and inspires you, to help you study and learn. In this way, AI could be used to level the playing field in education and help narrow socioeconomic gaps around the world." - Rana el Kaliouby

12 ENERGY & MATTER

*"Concerning matter, we have been all wrong.
What we have called matter is energy, whose
vibration has been so lowered as to be perceptible to
the senses. There is no matter." - Albert Einstein*

Mainstream science now tells us that everything is made up of particles that vibrate at various frequencies including rocks, plants, water, the air we breathe and every inanimate object we see. We exude energy and we absorb energy. Nothing is actually solid. Instead, objects are vibrating at frequencies that just make them appear solid. The things we cannot see (like gases in our atmosphere) are vibrating at high frequencies. Our limited sense of sight doesn't let us see the movement, or vibration of the particles. Just like light which vibrates from low frequency (radio) waves to high frequency (gamma) waves, we can only see a small portion of the visible light as colours.

Energy waves also "resonate" when they are smooth, regular, even and move in unison with the other energetic forms around it. This is what the natural form of energy looks like and as energy beings, our own vibrations should be the same.

If everything around us emits invisible waves that affect our energy, how do we interact with the world? The people we surround ourselves with and the environment we find ourselves in, can either deplete us or energize us. Our mind can also trigger emotions that can cause us to feel upset or stressed. So how do we control what goes in and out of our head? When we meditate, we become acutely aware of the problem of the numerous out-of-control thoughts. Where do all these thoughts come from? Some we don't even know are lurking in the background. When you wake from a lucid dream, it is always amazing how sometimes the dream seems to take on a life of its own and other times we can control the direction. Our mind is a mystery and it is a powerful tool. It affects everything in our lives including how we feel about ourselves. However, despite what we were told, our mind is not who we are and we need to be aware that our mind is a tool we need to command.

The field of physics has evolved over time. Classic physics was responsible for our fundamental understanding of the movement of the planets, of gravity, of how heat affects atoms, the chemical relationships between molecules, the nature of magnetism, how objects and projectiles move and what makes up the subatomic world. Calculus was originally included in physics in order to mathematically study changes in natural phenomena. The resulting discoveries of the Laws of Physics are not so much laws but observations of patterns, their descriptions and predictions of how nature behaves and interacts. Modern physics began in the early 20th century with Plank and Einstein, quantum mechanics and the General Theory of Relativity. These studies led to the description of nature at the atomic and subatomic levels and how the relationship of gravity with time and space is relative. The laws, no longer being absolute, can change depending on the players and position of the observer.

Most importantly was the discovery that the observed gravitational effects on and between masses, causes the bending or warping of time and space. The General Theory of Relativity implies time moves slower where gravity is stronger so that the further you get from the earth's surface, for example, the faster time passes. This is called the phenomena of "gravitational time dilation". So theoretically, those on the space station should age faster than those of us on earth, but they don't because of another phenomenon called "relative velocity time dilation". This is where time moves slower as you move faster. However, astronauts on the space station actually age slightly slower. The space station orbits so quickly that the velocity dilution wins out over the time dilution of the reduced gravitational pull. It is believed that if we were to move at the speed of light, time would stop. Scientists also hypothesize that time at the edge of a black hole would appear to stop because of the large gravitational pull. Therefore time travel is possible under certain conditions. It highlighted that the ideas of past, present and future are illusions. True reality is timeless. Einstein is quoted as saying that time *"is our way of making sense of growing up and growing old"*. While we exist in the third dimension of height, width and depth, time is considered by some as a fourth dimension.

So what we thought about time is not necessarily true. It is not an absolute constant but can change relative to mass and velocity. The Mayans and the ancient Hindu philosophers saw time as cyclical with everything repeating itself. Many eastern and western philosophers do not see time as an object but rather an illusion. They believe that the only time is the present moment, the past is a construct of the mind, just a memory. Physics and the clock measure of time, is a set of markers between a sequence of events that are as real as the lines of latitude and longitude on the earth. The marks of space between events must be observed and noted. As St. Augustine theorized, time does not exist if there is no one to witness it.

It is said that larger animals come to maturity more slowly than smaller animals. Therefore does an elephant experience a slower passing of time than a fruit fly? Perhaps time is like the waves on the ocean. You see each crest move forward toward the shore but in fact the water is not moving, but undulating in place. It just looks like the waves are moving. In the same way we are always in the present, stationary, moving along with the flow of time. We have never existed in the past or the future and never will. We are just here now.

At the atomic and subatomic levels of the universe, the String Theory postulated that everything in the universe consists of infinitesimally small vibrating strings. Left unproven, the Unified Field Theory then failed to tie together all the forces of the universe. However it is now generally accepted, according to the Quantum Field Theory, that all particles, the universe and all space, time and matter, consist of the excitation of quantum fields. Therefore all matter is made up of vibrating fields resonating at various frequencies. It is believed that the synchronization of the vibrations or resonance of these fields form various levels and types of consciousness. This Resonance Theory of Consciousness is thought to be the foundation of all physical reality.

It seems that all matter consists of energy fields in the state of vibration even if they appear solid. The movement of the energy is in the form of repeating waves or oscillations with a height (amplitude), width (time) and frequency (number of waves over a period of time) measured in Hertz (cycles or oscillations per second). Therefore we are no different in our physical makeup than everything else we can and cannot see. We are just more complex than other animals and inanimate objects because of the complexities of our biological energy pathways. We are all connected to everything and our energy frequencies communicate with everything that exists (matter, time, space and the universe).

"If you want to find the secrets of the universe, think in terms of energy, frequency and vibration." - *Nikola Tesla*

Energy is the medium with which we communicate fundamentally on an unconscious level with everything else. Our vibration can resonate, or not, within ourselves and with everything we are connected to. If we could realize this on a conscious level and synchronize in a healthy manner, not only can we be healed, but we can tell our bodies to live on in a positive way. Our cells do what they do through the messages they receive. They are already responsive to the frequencies and messages that we already generate. Therefore we can also consciously send our cells messages to affect our own biological development.

Strangely enough the newest frontier of physics and chemistry seem to indicate that through our synchronicity with universal energy, we can attain the power to create a change in our genetic expression. Because of the rules of entropy and tendency towards chaos, the Theory of Evolution requires that some form of organizing energy is needed for the evolution of a new species to develop. Explaining where this energy boost comes from, has been problematic. Jeremy England, from MIT, has proposed a new theory that the underlying principle in evolution is the theory of dissipation-driven adaptation of matter.

In an open system of entropy all matter acquires and dissipates energy. The better an organism is at receiving and giving off the energy it uses, the more efficient and survivable it is. According to England, *"We can show very simply from the formula that the more likely evolutionary outcomes are going to be the ones that absorb and dissipate more energy from the environment...on the way to getting there"*. Therefore organisms that resonate with the energy around them and gather more energy, then organize to make dissipation better, will outlive, out chance or have an evolutionary advantage over others.

One of the most efficient processes for gathering and dissipating energy is during reproduction. This process may be what drives all matter to organize and reproduce. It might not be because of "best and fittest" as had been believed. *"The formula based on established physics, indicates that when a group of atoms is driven by an external source of energy... it will gradually restructure itself in order to dissipate increasingly more energy"*, said England. The key is resonance with the environment in that, *"Particles tend to dissipate more energy when they resonate with the driving force"*. England's theory is gaining ground and has a lot of supporters. Many are now conducting experiments to test this new theory.

Humans, and all living things, for that matter are hardwired to detect vibrational frequencies through mechanoreceptors in the skin, visible light waves through the eyes and sound waves through the ears. The ability to detect energetic frequencies is an evolutionary feature to protect us. Harmful vibrations are choppy, uneven and not mirrored to frequencies found in nature. Examples include extreme or unpleasant sounds, tainted food, environmental pollutants and toxic relationships or people. Vibrations are messages in the form of energy waves. These invisible signals trigger us and then travel through our nervous system pathways and are processed by our brains.

A physicist by the name of Cohen, in 1972, developed a method for detecting and measuring the natural magnetic fields produced by various organs of the human body. It was determined that every organ has biomagnetic fields that produce specific pulsating frequencies. He found that the brain had the strongest emissions. The Institute of Heart Math however has done extensive work demonstrating that the heart's electromagnetic field is much stronger than that of the brain and can be measured in feet radiating out from the body.

Light also produces energy frequencies in a small range that we can see and a wider range of frequencies that we can't see. Photomultipliers, extremely sensitive phototubes, can detect light in the visible, ultraviolet and near infrared ranges at levels as small as an individual photon. With this, ultra weak light particles have been measured emerging from the hands and forehead. In fact all living organisms produce a continuous autoluminescence (glow). Some researchers are using this signal to determine the progression of aging, as damage to the body weakens our emissions.

Robert Becker, wrote a book called *The Body Electric*, where he mapped out the electrical resistance in the bodies of humans and other organisms. He found that our energetic anatomy closely resembles the same meridian pathways and acupuncture points used in traditional Chinese medicine. He also determined that the strength and shape of our energetic signals could be weakened or made stronger by outside forces from the environment and that these signals are the key to healing. He also believed that the phenomenon of extra sensory perception (ESP) occurred through the transmission of low frequency waves and that electromagnetic pollution is a greater risk to our health that we initially realized.

Many have since determined that every aspect of who we are is reflected in our biofield of frequencies. Heart Math is a method of connecting to the heart and activating "coherence" or synchronization of the heart to brain relationship. This group and others have found that the heart sends more signals to the brain than vice versa and that when a person achieves a harmonious link between the heart and the brain (resonance), the heart field becomes very large, leaps out from the person and affects everyone around it.

Heart vibes are particularly powerful. These are amplified by using physical techniques like increasing Qi (energy) by being in nature, eating quality foods, listening to music, inhaling pure essential oils, drumming, meditation, vocal toning, breath work, affirmations, connecting with the soul-spirit, doing qigong, activating the body's meridians and directing Qi energy through specific exercises with visualization and intention. It has also been determined that our frequencies are not only affected by physical transmitters, but also psychological changes. The active engagement of one's own bioenergetic field produces a compassionate presence infused with wisdom and power that facilitates restoration of health in others. Therefore cultivating emotions of compassion, empathy and gratitude, for example, will also positively affect one's own personal healing power. Dr. Moga was able to measure these shifts in the emission of magnetic fields from practitioners who were performing healing treatments.

Everything around us is a symphony of frequencies in many forms. The key to enjoying and benefiting from this concert of life, is to find a way to be in resonance with yourself and the world around you. Each season has vibrational properties that naturally align with the macrocosm and within our own microcosms. Therefore the power of resonance is about the vibes in us, those we were born with and those we cultivate through our physical and mental health. It is about the vibes in the environment that surrounds us and those relationships that support us. It is about how all these vibes "sync-up", balance and resonate with all the other vibes flowing through our reality. Our self-organized vibrational fields and complex resonance of these frequencies, make up our consciousness. Scientists studying the Resonance Theory of Consciousness, say *"shared resonance through specific neuron electrochemical firing patterns creates an electromagnetic field that may itself be the seat of macro-consciousness"*.

The Age of Reason was a rejection of everything that smacked of magic. We have been conditioned to only accept what can be proven in the laboratory. However there are many truths that cannot be tested using the scientific method. That does not mean they are not real. One time science accepted bodies of knowledge and known truths as accepted facts based on observation and validation of many people. The

Age of Reason ended that practice and made us question everything we thought we knew. Mankind actually regressed because of it. Reject the Grand Illusion and find out for yourself. Instead find your potential, run with it and shine.

"Your personal vibration or energy state is a blend of the contracted or expanded frequencies of your body, emotions and thoughts at any given moment. The more you allow your soul to shine through you, the higher your personal vibration will be." - Penney Peirce

13 THE INVISIBLE REALM

"The word "barzakh" from Qur'an 55:19-20 is an isthmus separating the material and spirit worlds... (it is an) intermediate realm, the middle state habitable by the human soul... (from Ibn Arabi)...

What does physics say about a supernatural world and our connection to it? Is this whole search for man's meaning just a giant conspiracy to keep us confused and controlled by our egos? Are the spiritual folks just deluded and looking for some sort of comfort? Or is there some objective peer reviewed evidence that points to a world more complex and more connected than we thought? Physics is the branch of science that originally meant "knowledge of nature". What we now know about energy and matter through physics, confirms that the unseen world of the invisible realm is real.

What confuses this matter is that what we were led

to believe just three hundred years ago, "if you can't see, hear, touch, taste or feel it, it doesn't exist". This is not true. So much for the Age of Enlightenment actually illuminating who and what we are. In fact there is more in our world that we cannot see, than what we can. According to Troy Erstling, *"In any given moment, your brain is processing about 400 billion bits of data, but you are only able to see about 2000 bits of that information, which is about 0.00000005%"*. So much of our world is beyond our senses. We only see things when light bounces off an object with frequencies within the range of visible light.

We know gravity exists when things fall to the earth but we can't actually see the force of gravity. Therefore we need to approach the examination of reality with more than our five senses and ordinary evidence. We need to apply logic and other types of clues. We need to ask ourselves, "what is the quality of the connection between man, nature and the invisible realm" above and beyond the vibration of particles? Like gravity, we know that radio and microwaves exist because we can hear the sounds or see the results. We also know that microbes and viruses exist because we were able to build microscopes, view them, create vaccines to fight them and watch the results unfold. We can't see aromas, flavours or sound as particles in the air but we can smell, taste and hear them. The same deductions hold true for magnetic fields, electrons and our WiFi signals. We cannot see the waves of energy they radiate but we are aware of the results of their activities as evidence that these things are real.

What about ideas, concepts, imagination, emotions and feelings like love? Nobody would say that these things don't exist just because they can't be measured and described by the five senses. These are things we know and detect by thought and perception. Messages from low vibrational frequencies, chemicals, nerve impulses and hormones within our biological processes, constantly feed us information without our conscious knowledge. These invisible processes affect our physical body, mental health and spiritual awareness.

"Love is a force more formidable than any other. It is invisible - it cannot be seen or measured, yet it is powerful enough to transform you in a moment, and offer you more joy than any material possession could." - Barbara De Angelis

So what do we know about these messages floating around us and inside us in the unseen world? To what extent do we interact with what is invisible? For example, how much of the invisible world do we rely on, when we are trying to determine the truth of something? Some people think they have no idea how to detect a lie. However, without even realizing it, subconsciously we have many ways to tell if something is true and we practice these skills all the time. Looking into a person's eyes can tell you how present they are, whether they themselves have a conviction about the information, or are just saying something in jest. Body language, voice inflection or pitch, tells us if the words are said with any particular emphasis or emotion that lends credence to the story. Prior familiarity with particular people and existing relationships can also influence what we detect in context of the personalities and group dynamics. If that person is considered reputable, knowledgeable and deemed worthy, then what they say must be true. We can sometimes know the truth by judging who is saying it. These exercises are done in the invisible realm and are real, not imaginary processes.

Then ultimately there is our energetic field that extends from us and mingles with the energy from everyone around us. We know that external energy vibrations exist because we can measure them. These invisible signals affect our biological fields and allow us to sense things. It is that energetic data that informs us in a "gut-feel" kind of way that we cannot always understand or express logically. These perceptions, our analytical thinking, observations of behaviours and recognition of patterns, are all clues we obtain from an invisible medium and involve the spirit realm.

Our spirit can also detect issues, connect to the universal energy and access information outside our bodies from the collective consciousness. This is how we recognize universal truths. We can feel the truth and what is real, by the way the information resonates with us. Truth feels right because it matches vibrational patterns that are familiar to our own spirit and feels synchronous with the extended invisible realm. According to Wikipedia, Theosophists believe that there is *"a compendium of all universal events, thoughts, words, emotions, and intent ever to have occurred in the past, present, or future in terms of all entities and life forms, not just human"*. These records supposedly exist on an invisible mental plane that some people can access and read. Perhaps this is where universal truths live.

In physics, the first law of thermodynamics says that energy can neither be created or destroyed. Therefore spirit entities that exist in the form of energy beings, are eternal. Belief in life, after death of the physical body, as the continuation of the soul consciousness, is a widely held view in religious, esoteric and metaphysical traditions around the world. Some believe that the soul goes to a specific place while others say it is reincarnated back into the physical world. The ancient Egyptians believed that parts of the soul had to undergo a series of tests and that rebirth was possible. The ancient Greeks and Romans believed that souls would be judged after they crossed the river to Hades and would end up in one of four places depending on how pure they were. In Norse beliefs the soul also could land in one of four places. In Judaic traditions the souls are "shades" without personality and everyone ends up in Sheol or Hades for a time, with the in-between journeys and final destinations dependent upon a judgment. Christian traditions have souls being resurrected to face judgment then ending up in Heaven or Hell.

The invisible realm also has entities apart from human souls, that exist mostly as energetic spirit beings. These are the angels and demons that are integral to most organized religions around the world. They live mostly beyond human detection but can become visible and exist in physical form when they choose to manifest it. The Roman Catholic doctrine says there are the pure spirits (angels) that are good, bad spirits that are separated from God (demons) and human spirits (souls separated from the body that are either saved or damned). In this aspect of the invisible realm, humans can be influenced by these complex, intelligent personalities that exist as spirits. Angels or demons, but not human souls, according to the Catholic church, can influence us through illumination by internal disclosure or subtle material manifestations. While some entities may encourage human minds in a positive way, we need to be aware of the negative forces. Greed for more money, for example, is used by demons to tempt mankind into behaving selfishly. The angels have great powers (with limitations as allowed by God) and knowledge to affect the material world and enter our thoughts and imaginations. They too have a vast influence in our lives.

Even if we do not realize it, we are forever caught in the middle of an invisible war that has been raging since creation. Satan and his minions are constantly seeking to drag the souls of men into eternal separation from God. Our biggest struggles as humans are not fought in the physical world of flesh and blood but with these powers and principalities of unseen forces. One can imagine an all encompassing spiritual battle being raged with all the entities playing their own parts. However even as the evil forces are present, opposing forces of good are there as well, shoring up whatever benevolent intentions we, as lesser beings, can muster, to give us the ultimate win. At least this is what the Catholic church tells us.

The spirit world however is not described in the context of religion. The unseen world is as real and complex as the physical world for most indigenous peoples. This is also true for those who adhere to metaphysical spiritualism where the spirits of the dead survive mortal life as a paranormal, supernatural, divine force. These can communicate with the living in various ways and can be invoked into contact with the living through shaman, clairvoyants, psychics, mediums and others. This is done using dance, sound, rituals, trance-states, seances, dreams, visions, independent writing and painting, divination and channeling as examples. Some claim the spirit world is the Home of the Soul and is a blissful place. For others the invisible world is no different than the physical world in that it mirrors similar experiences.

John Worth Edmonds stated in his 1853 work Spiritualism, "Man's relation spiritually with the spirit-world is no more wonderful than his connection with the natural world. The two parts of his nature respond to the same affinities in the natural and spiritual worlds." He asserted, quoting Swedenborg through medium-ship, that the relationship between man and the spirit world is reciprocal and thus could contain sorrow. Though ultimately, "wandering through the spheres" a path of goodness "is received at last by that Spirit whose thought is universal love forever." - Wikipedia

But how do you connect to that spirit within you? The heart-mind is that entity that competes with the brain-mind. The Heart is the original mind, the seat of the soul, where our authentic selves and power-connection to the universal spirit, lives. Our world puts great emphasis on the mind and believes it to be paramount to anything else. We have been told that we only exist because of our minds and that is who we are. We now know that is not true. Traditional knowledge keepers around the world know how to open that spirit connection to the invisible realm. The indigenous Shamans, the enlightened ones of the Indian and Dharmic eastern religions, religious mystics of Christian, non-Christian and Judaism and the wise masters of Taoism for example, are those who know "The Way".

"It is only with the heart that one can see rightly;

In traditional Chinese medicine, for example, there are five spirits connected to five body systems, each with unique attributes that flow in harmony with one another. They are Spleen-Yi, Lungs-Po, Kidneys-Zhi, Liver-Hun and Heart-Shen. The heart houses the Shen, controls the Shen and is the emperor or ruler over matters of the mind and spirit. That makes the heart the supreme spirit-mind. According to Diane Joswick:

"Chinese Medicine considers Shen to be one of the three treasures that constitute life: Jing, the essence; Qi, the life force; and Shen, the spirit. TCM views the spirit as an integral part of our health and our well being and cultivation of the spirit is considered essential for health maintenance... Chinese masters say it is through Shen that we radiate ourselves into the world. This spiritual radiance manifests as our wisdom, emotional well being, and ability to see all sides of an issue. Shen refers to that aspect of our being that looks to the universe around us, and is not focused on emotions. Shen draws our attention to the divine. It contributes to wisdom, virtue, and calmness, and maintains our whole being in order."

In the end physics has pointed us towards a new reality. This resonance with the universe is our power. It manifests itself in the way you view yourself and the world. The Grand Illusion would have us believe that this is all hog-wash and that if you can't see it, it doesn't exist. However science has confirmed what our ancestors have been trying to tell us and what the powers of this world have been trying to hide. We are so much more than a highly evolved ape and we have the power of the universe at our fingertips. We can heal, affect positive change and perform miracles. The secret lies in knowing that we are part of the unseen world and that wonderful things exist for us when we connect with the invisible realm. Don't let the illusionists convince you otherwise.

"Invisible things are the only realities; invisible things alone are the things that shall remain." - *William Godwin*

14 INTENTION

In the universe there is an immeasurable, indescribable force which shamans call intent, and absolutely everything that exists in the entire cosmos is attached to intent by a connecting link. - Carlos Castaneda

Adults who are seeing the reality behind that mask of illusion and are trying to tell others, are being hated and misunderstood. Some wonder if they were conceived on the wrong planet. This madness is something that we will have to endure for a time. If we look at how young children cope, we can re-learn how to be present, take each moment as it comes, be and do what feels right in the moment. You are the light that will guide the world and expose the darkness for what it is. You are needed now more than ever. You are here at this particular time in our world for a critical purpose. As long as we keep our hearts and minds free from bad thoughts, we can be assured that our actions and words will flow from the best intentions. As a human being, that is the best we can do. We are all heroes, heroines and warriors, each in his and her own right.

One of the first things I learned about acupuncture was to set my intention at the tip of the needle. What does that mean? I knew it was an important lesson, but it would be years before I realized just what that meant. Whole books have been written about how important intention is. Then as I learned Therapeutic Touch®, I experienced how intention combined with compassion was a key ingredient for healing. According to Wayne Dyer, if you are connected to the power of intention, you radiate energy that affects everyone around you, like ripples in a pond. When you see that your intention brings about your desires, your belief in its abundance grows and creates a fountain of power. You start to manifest your world by co-creating it with intention.

"The power of intention is the power to manifest, to create, to live a life of unlimited abundance, and to attract into your life the right people at the right moments." - Wayne Dyer

Staying focused on a detailed intention can be difficult. However, many people have learned how to fine tune this to an art. Visualization can help as you watch the desired state unfold and manifest into reality in real time, while remaining in a state of thankfulness. The key here is not the question but focusing on the answer coming true, right there and then. No hoping for it to happen in the future. Know that it is done and feel deep gratitude for that. It also helps to be in balance everyday and have a dedicated spiritual practice. Some call it grounding but however you do it, it helps to connect to the earth's energy, the spirit within you and the omnipresent spirit that surrounds you. Without that grounding, you can get pulled into the emotions and drama and become unbalanced. This is exhausting. Practising the art of gratitude every day also helps to boost energy and passion. This becomes easier over time.

According to traditional Chinese medicine, Qi is a form of energy that is our life force. It infuses the body, runs through the meridians and when it is plentiful and flows properly, we are OK. The only way to extend our lives, is to supplement the qi we were born with through the air we breathe and the food we eat. This can be done through what we eat, how we move and what we think. Being in nature supplies high energy directly to our lungs especially when the air is clean.

We can also conserve and concentrate that acquired post heaven qi by learning to be calm and positive through mediation, for example. This is a good way to check in, pull back the curtains of what is going on in the mind, gauge our emotions and analyze the inner state through introspection. Qigong or yoga as a form of exercise, also teaches us how to pull more energy from our surroundings. Then slow, deep breathing helps us make more efficient use of qi. In this way we can maximize the food and air to give us the most nutrients.

According to the old ways, sickness is linked to imbalances in the mind and are physical manifestations of emotional dis-ease. Well-being depends on the environment, our living conditions, our relationships, our social structures, our support systems, social justice, housing availability, food scarcity as well as a good diet and exercise. We have the ability to do what we need to thrive naturally and easily like the Immortals, Sages, Achieved Beings and Naturalists who lived to over one hundred years. When these ancient beings got sick they *"...guided properly the emotions and spirit and re-directed the energy flow...to heal the condition.",* Then they used herbs, herb-wines, acupuncture, moxibustion and kept a clear mind. They integrated the mental, physical and spiritual aspects of their being with exercise, meditation, a balanced diet, at regular times and maintained a pure conscience.

"Every object, including human organs, have a natural healthy vibratory rate referred to as "resonance." If a part of the body begins to vibrate out of resonance or harmony, it creates what we term dis-ease." - D. Takara Shelor

Rising up into our power can be like the smoke from fire or incense, that ascends into the atmosphere, dissipating into the heavens. This may describe a spiritual shift, revelation, epiphany or mountain top experience that changes a person forever. It could also refer to a new or renewed faith, an answer to prayer or even a complete conversion of faith and beliefs. It is also a conscious preparation to develop a more uplifting attitude through study, education, meditation, yoga, religious or spiritual practices. In this sense it often means adopting or changing towards a more interiorly aware, or closer relationship to a higher power.

Rising up to claim power can also be an upward movement of one's conscious awareness to adopt a wider view, bigger picture and higher understanding. It is an elevated spiritual state that requires a connection with a higher power and a sense of knowing that comes from beyond the physical, mental and emotional states. It also involves vibrational frequencies, the state of our energetic wave forms and increasing the volume, pitch and intensity of our own personal vibrational state.

The sense of self comes from the harmonious vibrations that we feel as the seer behind our eyes. This can happen when we quiet ourselves and become aware of the music of ourselves, as a small still voice in our hearts. This spontaneous self-organization of the expression of our DNA blueprint of millions of oscillating fields, is our perception that "I am Me". The more we pay attention, it becomes apparent that the key to knowing ourselves lies in the synchronicity with the universal high frequency energies in everything. We are not just a Me. We are the eyes of the higher power looking out on itself. This is the greatest of all secrets that has been hidden from us.

Practically speaking when we really listen, and see others, the dynamics of caring people gathering together, opens up a shared energy field. When the goal is to always help, not harm, be open and loving, intention is powerful. It is even more than that when love and compassion are added. Love is actioned through compassion and you can't be compassionate if you don't love. Otherwise judgment takes over and you don't see others as they really are. It is important to hear the stories of struggle, triumph and defeat and see the strength and beauty in each person. It is appropriate to be in awe of each person we meet in regard to the totality of what each person has had to endure and overcome. This is how the angels see us and in this state of reverence for others, spirit allies come in and commune with us and our compassionate circle of others. It is a powerful experience where high level frequencies are supercharged and each person comes away from the circle with new insights and inspiration.

The power of intention is the power to manifest, to create, to live a life of unlimited abundance, and to

When surrounded by caring supportive people, learning, being conscious of our mind's activities, moving through the world as a healthy, high frequency individual, being true to yourself and seeking our soul self, we are capable of impacting those around us in a positive way. It is analogous to carrying a lantern, keeping it well supplied with oil, keeping the wick trimmed and our own light burning brightly, so that we can ignite the torches of those we meet along the way. Our reach goes beyond time and space as those who are positively impacted by us, pay it forward. As those others vibrate at a higher level, they touch those in their lives. The good intentions we begin can create ripples that can heal the world. This is The Way and how you do that is your own path.

It is in that mix, that individuals and groups experience intention fuelled by compassion, supported by spirit, through the gateway of gratitude. This is really a three legged stool that supports our words and the detailed vision of what we want to create for ourselves and others. Using intention and manifesting our power is not a special calling. It comes naturally as we learn to see ourselves as something more, connected to everyone and everything. Creating positive change is the result of caring about others and our planet. The process is a journey of self discovery to becoming whole and recognizing the goodness within oneself. The result of this combination based in love, creates a high frequency healing bubble filled with, what I call, supercharged intention.

"Where you put your hands, is where energy goes...Where you focus your mind is where you boost energy and heal...To meld with Tao is to reach immortality..." - Tao I (The Way of All Life) by Master Zhi Gang Sha

Saving the earth requires a love that is not just a strong affection or feelings for someone. It must be strong enough to put others ahead of itself, believe the best in people, give them the benefit of doubt, as well as put one's own self in high esteem. Love treats others, self and the environment, with respect and reverence. Saving the planet will need a different approach to what has gone on before. The power of love will need to be channelled in new ways, compounded at the very least, by three levels of existence. It is imperative to learn what it means to rise up into our true power, if we want to make meaningful change. It is time to let go of the lies and illusions and harness the knowledge of who we are, belief in our capabilities with love, compassion and empathy, clear minds, healthy bodies and a connected spirit.

"The highest intention comes from love and compassion ... when our intentions come from a place of love and compassion then we have the power of the

universe... Intentions compressed into words enfold magical power." - Deepak Chopra

When we are "in the zone", as described above, we are protecting and optimizing our health, our vibration resonates with nature and the creator-spirit. In this state we are able to increase the qi of our bodies, minds and spirits and get the wrinkles out of our own energy bodies. On this good solid foundation, we know we are loved and lovable, we radiate good energy vibrations wherever we go. We cause others to feel hope, happiness, optimism and belief in something greater than themselves. We can spread love to others.

Ultimately we will rise up into our true selves as we navigate the difficulties and challenges in the world. We can use the external crises to source that inner strength of spirit to transform ourselves. Taking what is wrong on the outside and changing ourselves on the inside, beyond the limitations of our rational minds, into our higher consciousness, is the kind of "Rise Up" that Caroline Myss calls "Defying Gravity". Everyday challenges become lessons in creative problem solving to strengthen our spiritual muscles. Over time you see there is nothing you can't handle and that you are so much more powerful than you could imagine. Anything is possible. Here, rise up is a kind of resilience that comes from a connection with universal forces. Here is the proving ground for who we are, where we came from and why we are here. This is the ultimate rising up into our true nature.

Over time, the spiritual capacity for internal elevation grows stronger, moving us past the point of destruction. This is where we realize that there is more to life than our immediate situations and we get a glimpse of a bigger picture. This is where you realize that all things work together for the good for all involved, beyond what our small minds can't comprehend. Some people experience an infusion of unconditional love that goes beyond the capabilities of human love. At that point, the realization is, that we as humans, are a conduit of and are part of the essence of life itself. This allows us to shift focus from the immediacy and finality of the now, to the eternal. Rising up into our power, incorporates the broadest range of actions, attitudes, beliefs and supports needed to care for ourselves and deal with our own crises. It allows us to escape the low level, dense vibrations of hate, vengeance and fear that traps us in a hell of our own making.

"A radical inner transformation and rise to a new level of consciousness might be the only real hope we have in the current global crisis..." - Stanislav Grof

The highest frequencies we can experience occur when we resonate with love, compassion, empathy, forgiveness and gratitude. These vibrations allow us to transcend the material, visible world. In this state we can experience joy, even in the most difficult circumstances, as a resident of the kingdom of God within us as our higher self. Changing the world for the better, from this vantage point, is activism on steroids. When virtue is supported by courage, intelligence and faith, we are aligned with best intentions and the goals of the universe. This connection to our higher self, grounds us and enables us to access our inner human superpowers. Knowing who we are and being our true selves in the world is our purpose and destiny. Then rising up into this power, takes us beyond revolution to personal, individual and collective evolution where we will not only survive the chaos, but elevate all of mankind and usher in a new and better world.

"It is our purpose and destiny to live in conscious oneness with our world, be present and know that our true identity is in the reflection of the divine. When your non-persona can tap into your passion and your actions are directed by love, inspiration and enthusiasm, your work will resonate in alignment with the goals of the universe. This is the secret to knowing your life purpose. A purpose that you can fulfill every day you have the courage to be true to what you know and what is right. In this way you will change the world with more power than any one person could ever imagine." - SG Williams

15 THE NATURE OF MAN

"Human nature is complex. Even if we do have inclinations toward violence, we also have an inclination to empathy, to cooperation, to self-control." - Steven Pinker

The argument about the Nature of Man is varied and as old as the early philosophers. Some say that the attributes of man are a matter of genes (nature) while others say it is the result of conditioning (nurture). Some argue that the nature of man is fixed (innate) while others say it is changeable (depending on circumstances). Socrates believed that humans are best suited for reasoning, that the soul is divided between that aspect of ideas and its desires and passions. In Chinese Confucianism man is considered essentially good with tendencies toward virtue but can act bad against his nature, if harm or injury pushes him in that direction. Other Chinese schools of thought say that man is evil and selfish by nature but is only good as the result of abundance in his environment, training, discipline and conditioning. In Christianity, man was created in the image of God and some said the nature of man is a microcosm that reflects the universe. Pico argued that man was free to choose his own essence. Aquinas believed that the soul aspect, while united with the body, was immortal and could act independently of the body.

"Human nature comprises the fundamental dispositions and characteristics - including ways of thinking, feeling, and acting - that humans are said to have naturally. The term is often used to denote the essence of humankind, or what it 'means' to be human. This usage has proven to be controversial in that there is dispute as to whether or not such an essence actually exists." - Wikipedia

Our human-ness, humanity and the nature of mankind is the collective of all the base characteristics that separate us from animals. These attributes include complex reasoning, problems solving, language, introspection and memory along with consciousness, emotions and the ability to plan and act from a moral perspective. We are in the middle, a hybrid being between the beasts and the divine. The virtues of hope, love, acceptance, caring, compassion, fairness, morality, creativity and a sense of purpose, are things we chose, as higher beings, to express our authentic higher self.

"I have given you neither a determined place, nor a face of your own, says the creator, nor any particular gift, O Adam, so that your place, your face and your gifts you may conquer and possess by yourself. Nature encloses other species in laws established by me. But you, whom no boundary limits, by your own free will, in whose hands I have placed you, define yourself." Giovanni Pico della Mirandola from his Discourse on the Dignity of Man

It is this spirit of consciousness and connection to the divine that keeps us from devolving to our base animalistic nature. We are beings that collectively decided, or were imbibed with the wisdom, to choose, support and force ourselves into a model of living that would better align with our divine nature. This was the impetus to form civilizations with societies, laws, rules and governments to protect that collective higher nature of humanity. Everything that our civilization has come to value, respect and enforce and pass on to our children, is a means to ensure the continuation of our species into the future generations. We continue that tradition by trying to make the world more inclusive, protecting our vulnerable and caring for others. Tapping into our divine nature and practising ethics, morality and the virtues are what has given us the skills to survive.

"Indeed, human nature is a tricky thing. We are, after all, the only species who can reflect on our own nature, thus providing both the capacity to transcend

Most religions teach that man has the capacity to be good or bad. That we can easily slip into the dark side when aroused by negative emotions. The dark side in us can then vibrate and resonate with inherent non human evil energy that coexists with good energies. If we are depressed, angry and upset and allow ourselves to sit in that dark place too long, or feel the excitement of hate stir as it can, we can be co-joined with powerful external negative forces that can consume us. This is one aspect of human nature we must always guard against. It takes more willpower to do what is right than to do what is wrong when tempted by ill gotten gains and benefits, in the shadows, where we think nobody can see.

Others say there is no such thing as evil. Instead dark forces in the world are sometimes considered just a natural part of our existence to balance the polarities of light found in the universe. Many who believe in the unseen entities are aware of forces for good and evil far greater than anything that man can imagine. Every culture tells stories of its angels and demons. Sometimes it just takes serendipity of an unfortunate nature, to cause non-human elementals to manifest in destructive ways by the inadvertent introduction of evil into our space. Evil allowed to flow in the human form can conjure an entity with more power than just a human alone.

The draw towards our animal nature can be intoxicating. We feel the support of our pack as we run free as wolves, devouring what and whomever we please. Once those signals of conscience are deadened enough, the base instincts for survival, the adrenaline of the hunt and the fight makes us feel alive. Our base sexual impulses, desire for pleasure, feelings of belonging to the pack and the need to feel superior can be overwhelming. These traits run deep in us as do our fight and flight responses. The pack allows a person to feel the benefits of the superiority of their group, feeds the ego's drive for self-importance and for many, the choice to follow rather than lead, not think and just obey, is comforting. It is these animalistic innate instincts that reside in the amygdala (lizard brain) that makes us react with fear, aggression or dominance.

Anything that challenges the beneficial, benevolent, positive aspects of human nature, threatens our long-term future. If our base animal selves are expressed over those of the divine, the unemotional, uncaring, greedy, self-centred, violent, hateful, murdering, morally bankrupt, logic driven characteristics will become our most dominant features. We will no longer be human, our humanity will fade out. A lesser mankind with complex analytical abilities, devoid of consciousness, heart and soul, will become, not just an animal, but a smart calculating beast that behaves like a machine.

That robot-likeness devoid of a conscience, gives man the freedom to be ruthless in the name of better efficiencies. We will no longer serve the preservation of the good for all humanity, but the needs of economy, progress, greed and the domination of one individual over another. This leads us to a society that breeds control of others, subjugation of others and the destruction of others for the sake of a few. This is how fascist government regimes are born and that is what is happening on a world-wide scale now. The acceptability and lack of objection to having AI displace humans, without studying the consequences, could mean a world lost in the sea of mobbing, machines and fascism. The survival of our collective humanity is not possible unless we practice our higher virtues and guard against getting caught up and consumed by our lower base animal-selves, in emotionally based ego wars of jealousy and retribution, for example.

The dawn of the end of man's higher nature, looks like a world of injustice, discrimination and domination of others through deception, lies, theft, hate, bulling, mobbing and genocide. Every time we dehumanize and devalue someone else through stereotypes and gossip or act out of fear for our survival, as the ego often does, we lose part of our own humanity. As we pit one group against the other and support divisive politics instead of cooperation, we become more ingrained into the base side of our animal nature, losing contact with our conscience and divinity.

"Through the unique human capacity of conscious will-power, at the juncture when thoughts turn to action, the soul can either capitulate to the siren calls of its lower nature ... and egotistical demands, or can restrain and detach from these cravings and with the divine assistance, ascend to its positive condition..."

"But there is conflict... people commonly vacillate... wondering which way to go, or whether to move at all.. (this is) a common condition in human nature, where both the negative side and positive side engage in a sort of tug-of-war with man in the middle. We all experience it and often suffer the consequences. It can be a powerfully negative combination or the proving ground where the heat of tests and trials distills out the lower base elements and concentrates the higher spiritual elements of human nature." - Ned Walker, bahaiteachings.org

We have an immense capability for good from our higher self while the lower-self risks driving all living things to extinction and destroying our planet. The direction we take as a human race depends on the individual's choice to behave in ways that will either elevate or debase their nature. The higher virtues, ethics, morality, kindness, caring, empathy and loving others takes effort, work, practice and a dedicated choice. The lower behaviours of competition, fear, dominance and pleasure come easily without thought or planning. Without some effort, energy and positive change on the part of the individual, our world will fall into chaos.

"There runs a strange law through the length of human history – that men are continually tending to undervalue their environment, to undervalue their happiness, to undervalue themselves. The great sin of mankind, the sin typified by the fall of Adam, is the tendency, not towards pride, but towards this weird and horrible humility." - G. K. Chesterton

There are positive actions we can take. We can make a significant impact as individuals. We have the power to reclaim our humanity and heal society of its toxic culture, by practising those attributes that make us uniquely human. It is the human side of our mammal-ness that will enable us to change the world for the better. How each of us responds to the daily siren call of egocentric, self-serving behaviours, affects us all. With the decline in the influence of world religions, we need to make a concerted effort to focus on what is good and rout out those things that have caused a decline in our evolution. We need to preserve, protect and increase mankind's divine attributes that keeps us grounded in being human. It is the true authentic and divine aspect of the nature of man that elevates us above our animal instincts and anchors us in love. That is a critical factor in the future survival for ourselves, our children and the planet.

Practising our connection to the highest frequencies of our creator, gives us the ability to step away from the internal battles and see what is really happening. Our ego operates at a different wavelength and tends to reside in our mind, or at least is reinforced with our mind. In order to act within the guideposts considered normal in society, it takes a fair amount of negotiation and harmony between the three aspects of animal nature, the ego and our higher self. How we move through life depends on our successes in the way we manage these. People who choose to be courageous and speak up about wrongdoing are individuals who protect, nourish, grow and express their higher selves. They do so often at a great cost to themselves in the face of opposition and hate. They are folks who educate themselves to avoid being manipulated and adding to evil in the world. They are also often Truth Tellers who have a need to seek the facts and be true to themselves. These are those people who will prevent the end from happening and succeed in turning the world back around towards a better beginning.

"Through consciousness, our minds have the power to change our planet and ourselves. It is time we heed the wisdom of the ancient indigenous people

and channel our consciousness and spirit to tend the garden and not destroy it." - Bruce Lipton

Again, these ideas on the Nature of Man are not what the powers creating the illusions want us to know. Quantum Entanglement in physics describes how a group of particles become acquainted by interacting together in the same space in a way that they become indistinguishable, appearing as one entity in a quantum state. Then when the particles are separated, even over long distances, they still cannot be distinguished independently from the whole. We too are more than our individual cells when we resonate and therefore tap into a collective power of creation. We are an Us who is integral to the shared consciousness of God, Spirit, Tao, Brahman or higher power. We have always been associated with that same energy that created us in the first place, inseparable as in a quantum state. Therefore it is up to us to accept this wonderful insight and use our power wisely by "living correctly", in harmony with the seasons and all the earth's inhabitants. We are the God particle.

Cycle of Nature

The cycle of the earth breathes the energy of birth, growth and decline. We too undergo a cycle of transformation that is beautiful and perfect.

Awaken to this rebirth and become aware of your magnificence. Love yourself wholly and accept the spirit of the universe that is at the core of who you are. Be in awe of every moment and see the magic in the ordinary. Cherish what you behold with new eyes.

Feel the peace of gratitude envelop you. Listen to your heart and seek your true self by dissolving the fog of the world. Be free. Know that you are perfect just as you are, wonderfully made and specially purposed.

*Love the Earth. Embrace joy even in the most difficult times and know that you are loved, even if it is not a love from this world. Laugh, sing, dance and heal. Watch as your passions fulfill your deepest desires. Know that you, as a **divine being**, can create the world of your dreams.*

- SG Williams

16 Conclusions

I believe people do sense that our world is one big fantastical tale of deception. The things we have been taught are not 100% true. It is the stories with just a hint of truth that make the best and most convincing lies. However, in all fairness we were not ready to see or understand much of what we are now learning. Many people will never be able to accept any deviations from the common narratives because the truth is too unsettling. How could all the experts we trusted be so wrong for so long? We probably knew more eons ago, about the grand picture of the universe, and who we are, than we do now. I imagine we were also smarter in ancient times than we are now.

Like Adam in the Eden story, we realized we had knowledge and most likely wanted more. However, I imagine that we would have become much more difficult to control, as we grew in wisdom. There are stories that have surfaced where the rulers (gods) complained about man's intelligence and took efforts to reduce that. It seems some efforts may have been through air pollution, others by creating illness and making us stressed. All these things affect our mental capabilities. Then perhaps by burying the true stories, reinforcing and rewarding our compliance to the hierarchies and teaching the value of obedience, were all part of that effort to make us more docile. Mankind's quest for learning was most likely met with resistance and was thwarted in a number of ways.

Instead of seeing the big picture and looking upward, man became focused on drilling down into the minutia of earth bound mysteries. Scientists took apart everything to understand the component parts and how they worked. Every rabbit hole took us further and further into silos of information. We did discover infinitesimal details about so many things. It was and is wonderful. It made us heady with pride, self-righteousness and filled with judgment about how smart we are. In the eons of distraction with the material world, seeking information and navel gazing, we forgot to see the patterns in the whole and the beauty of the connections. We should have been looking outward for answers as to who and why instead of just how.

Somewhere and somehow, the shadows in earth's vibration became darker, denser and more base as people became less family and community centered. The greed of fewer well connected rulers redirected resources to themselves. Cities became bigger metropolises, slavery and feudalism impacted freedoms, rights and man had to work harder to survive. Wars and unrest over power and resources became the constant background noise. Man wanted to live like and look like gods. Mankind did not want to share the credit, for developing the world, with anyone but himself. Admitting that a higher power had any role in man's elaborate real-estate schemes for entire continents, would mean that man would have to be more honourable and less scrupulous, perhaps. In a secular world, nobody was watching or holding mankind accountable. Everything done in the shadows was fair play.

People who knew the old stories, traditions and ways of connecting to our higher selves, were targeted and silenced. This was done by the killing of heretics in the crusades, the attempted genocide of indigenous people world-wide, burning of our wise women as witches and distorting the teachings of true masters and holy people. The folks that remained were then marginalized by slander, prejudice and scorn. This included anyone practising traditional medicine and healing modalities. Man's connection to the spirit world and his support of the unseen helpers, underwent a divorce. Their teachings were no longer deemed credible and were forgotten by accepted mainstream thinking.

This was done intentionally by many nations all over the world. Who would do such a thing and why? For this program to be so widely effective from the genocide of indigenous peoples everywhere to the Jews during the Holocaust, seems like one huge terrible conspiracy, not something that happened by chance. I do not believe that mankind is capable of doing this on their own. Somebody, a higher power would have to be behind it. We are just not that good at keeping secrets and working well together with others. This is especially true of a group of ambitious men with power. They could not pull off the kind of conspiracies at play in our world without falling out with each other and their alliances, out of greed and suspicion.

I believe it is more likely that more advanced intelligent beings use human groups and individuals as puppets to carry out their agendas. I suspect that before ancient civilization began, there was war between the ruling gods, each with their own territories, vying for control over mankind. This war started long ago and continues today. I suspect that some of these gods cared about us, some hated us and some may have been indifferent. Some of the gods nurtured us and gave us advanced knowledge, while other gods thought it foolhardy. Some even mated with our kind and changed our genetics. Some hoped we would grow in wisdom while others thought we might just squander our education and destroy ourselves. Some may have just seen us as slaves and work horses, a means to an end and did not care what happened to us once their own goals were achieved, whatever they might be.

Our real history may be the root cause of the crises we are now experiencing. Over time as mankind was made to forget who he truly was. Then as many lost that connection to the divine, we started to devolve. This can be seen when our leaders do not care about the vulnerable and society does not see injustice as an issue. At an even deeper level, the ignorance of, complacency towards and willingness to knowingly induce these societal issues, dives into the realms of true evil. This is when people intentionally take something from, lie or act in ways to cause harm to others, just to enrich or benefit themselves. Worse are corrupt people, within our institutions that we are supposed to trust, who weaponize their positions of power to defame others, break laws, steal, cheat, abuse others and trample the vulnerable without consequence. When man sees those with less power, as unworthy lesser beings, not deserving of respect or consideration, this is proof that a reign of evil is the predominant force in the world.

There is something bigger happening here than just bullying by police, neighbours, work colleagues, rogue policing gone bad, a failed justice system and the corruption of those who are in positions of trust in our institutions. The "something more" points to the presence of evil and the seeming lack of conscience or a soul in people who commit such harmful acts against others or stand by and watch without intervening. This is psychological warfare at its worst. To accuse and demean others, push them out of neighbourhoods, rob them of their homes, financial security, jobs, feelings of self worth and harming people's mental wellness, is just wrong. Those that stand by, watch and enable the hate, have no mercy and will completely gut their victim until they have nothing left, even urging them to leave this world prematurely. Nobody can convince me that this is not evil.

"Evil is an attack against human spiritual development and enlightenment. All evil, badness, neurosis – It has one motive and one motive only, which is to destroy- To destroy your chance of arising above yourself." - Vernon Howard

In the end I think that the good gods who cared for us in ancient times, lost big-time in the struggle for dominion over earth and mankind. Our ancestors went to a lot of work to carve the origins of our existence into stone and hide our stories on scrolls that were then buried in deep caves. They wanted us to know the truth because they probably knew what was coming. They wanted us to eventually find out the truth to give us hope and a chance to succeed. It is precisely because this knowledge was so important, these artifacts and ancient stories were attacked by churches and states, banned, destroyed and then trivialized as myths. New stories were created and taught to distort the truth and became part of the Grand Illusion. The history of man has been one endless struggle against these powers of darkness.

Slowly the truth was and is being revealed. The mask has been removed so that many are seeing the true face of mankind. Many are starting to remember, in the core essence of their souls, what we were made to forget. Over the centuries, prophets and messengers were sent to remind us where we came from, who we are and to not lose hope. Our creator, the source of all life, from which everything came into being, wants us to know that we matter. We do have someone(s) watching over us. It is not just angels and saints from the invisible realm but based on the multitudes of UFO or UAP sightings, higher beings or advanced relatives in this physical world, are also checking in.

Points of light and hope are breaking up this darkness, however. The hierarchies and inaccessibility of knowledge, that gave some more power than others, has been levelled. The prevalence of the internet has democratized information. More people can access what had once been unavailable and are now sharing, considering, analyzing and integrating new information into their sphere of knowledge. Ordinary people are educating themselves, finding a platform and making their voices heard. The speed of change in the knowledge of the masses of people, all over the world, has greatly accelerated. At the same time there has been an unmasking of the illusions. Many are re-connecting with those spirit centered individuals that have been marginalized and are listening to the knowledge they impart. Modern science and medicine are just starting to catch up to the advanced ways and practices from so long ago. Slowly our traditional knowledge is being recaptured and reclaimed.

Counter-acting this ability to achieve our optimal selves, is the prevalence of disease and stress. The most devastating dis-ease in the world today is the attack on self esteem and the manifestation of self-hate. We are constantly being told and reminded that we are never enough. The magazines show people always well dressed in beautiful homes. Movies and television, even when trying to display real life, do not. Neither do our Facebook feeds where we pose as our glamorous selves and post a fantasy world. It's hard not to compare ourselves to others. The world has become increasingly narcissistic. People are more and more selfish and the culture is a belief in scarcity not abundance. We clamour to get ahead of others and take from others. People are not always kind, some spread hate and some bully others to make us feel smaller, to combat their own issues with self worth. This perpetuates this dis-ease and a pandemic of self-loathing. These events are the signs, signatures, outcomes of the Grand Illusion working as intended.

"Over the years I have come to realize that the greatest trap in our life is not success, popularity or power but self-rejection...When we have come to believe in the voices that call us worthless and unlovable, then success, popularity and power are easily perceived as attractive solutions...Self-rejection is the greatest enemy... it contradicts the sacred voice that calls us the "Beloved". Being the Beloved constitutes the core truth of our existence." - Henri Nouwen

Many of us have been so deeply hurt and injured, that the thought of being healthy, healed and helping others, seems impossible. I want to acknowledge that some pits are so dark, professional help and support is a must. We have all suffered trauma in some way. As individuals we are all impacted differently, some more severely than others. Many have lost their way, given in to the belief that they are not valuable and have resorted to self harming behaviours. Please seek help. You are a valuable soul and worth it. Many of the most powerful people are those who have come out of a dark place and survived. Some call it the dark night of the soul. Those folks are uniquely able to help others surrounded in darkness because they know the place and landscape. If you are such a person suffering, know that the deeper the pain etches into your soul, the greater joy you will be able to contain and the greater compassion you will feel for others, once you get to the other side.

There is hope and a path forward but it is not by doing what we have always done. It requires a different approach infused with power, unity and sacrifice. It is insane to keep doing the same things for eons and expect a different outcome. War, hate, fighting and protesting from that same base of anger, will not change the world anymore. The earth and its inhabitants have crossed a tipping point of no return. If we can get beyond self-hate and begin to believe we are worthy. If we can see a tiny bit of light shining from beyond that pit and just hold on. The way to a better world is not beyond our reach.

"Do not let the memories of your past limit the potential of your future. There are no limits to what you can achieve on your journey through life, except in your mind... Believe in your infinite potential..." - Roy T. Bennett, The Light in the Heart

What is happening politically all over the world, is uncovering, in a big way, what is wrong in the world. For too long we have propped-up a world of false and superficial peace that denies the existence of the darkness. We have all collectively played a role in this. The true face of humanity is not the beautiful picture that the Grand Illusion has painted. To bring about balance, we need to love and listen to the messengers who are expressing their pain. We need to allow the painful words to move us towards introspection of what is dark in us. Like yin and yang, we are both dark and light and the two must be in balance. True peace cannot come until all things are reconciled. This applies to both our internal life and our exterior world. In darkness we are negative, paralyzed and asleep. In light we are positive, active and awake.

While darkness is growing, at its darkest hour, it will always flow back again towards increasing light. This is the nature of yin and yang. This is our guarantee of hope. The global unrest, the inability to know truth from lies and the ongoing effects of the recent pandemic, are all telling us it is time. It is time to shake off the coldness, hibernation, protectionism, and fear that represent the winter-water elements in the world. We need to prepare our hearts and souls for change. We need to begin or continue to question the norms, customs, expectations and beliefs that others impose on us. We each have the power to change the world. We are not only inextricably connected to our physical environment as science outlines in quantum physics, but we are also one with the invisible consciousness of the universe. Therefore our thoughts and actions not only affect our own health but the well-being of others and how the future is manifested.

"When you want something, all the universe

We are powerful spiritual entities, living a human experience. We must guard ourselves against people who consistently mess with our lovely mind-garden. We need to know, remind ourselves and tell others that the Grand Illusion and this world as it seems to appear, is not real. This material world that we struggle with and are able to see is only a fraction of the real world. Most of our world is in the unseen realms. Keeping this knowledge in the forefront of our minds, being aware of our mind chatter and monitoring our emotions, helps us keep balanced and connected to these universal forces. We are very important. So much so that the angels bow down to us, watch over us and help us. Why is it that even the angels are honoured by our presence? As Alan Watts has said in *The Book, On the Taboo Against Knowing Who You Are,* "you're IT". You are not the ME looking out at everything else. You are IT (everything that was, is and ever will be as David Icke says) looking out onto the world of everything that is.

"You are not IN the universe, you ARE the universe, an intrinsic part of it. Ultimately, you are not a person, but the focal point where the universe is becoming conscious of itself. What an amazing miracle." - Eckhart Tolle

The good news is that what you look for in earnest,

you will find. Ask the universal higher power (even if you don't believe). Ask for verification that God exists. Pose your questions from wherever you are on your journey towards truth. Identify those things you have been told that never felt right and take another look. Examine your doubts and get to the bottom of your truth and clarify your own reality. The important message of all these stories is that we each need to work out our own salvation for whenever and however the end should come. Don't be discouraged by predictions of impending doom. Don't be afraid. Don't believe everything you hear. Keep looking. Find the answers for yourself. Find your truth. Cling to that truth. Know you are a beautiful, unique, powerful and worthy being. Know you are not alone and find your tribe. Know that you can and will, withstand and prevail against the powers of darkness in these last days.

"Believe nothing, no matter where you read it, or who said it, no matter if I have said it, unless it agrees with your own reason and your own common sense."
- Buddha

ABOUT THE AUTHOR

SG Williams is a wellness specialist, author and publisher with experience in scientific research, technology, long-term care of the elderly, traditional holistic healing and acupuncture. She believes in simplicity, authenticity, the need to find inner peace and keeping the wonder of life alive by paying attention to our surroundings. She sees every person as unique and specially created with something important to teach us. In her opinion it is imperative for everyone to have access to healthy communities, where people can be appreciated for who they are, free from injustice, discrimination and able to access the basic needs and rights they deserve. She believes in speaking up and telling the truth when it is needed to benefit and educate others.

OTHER BOOKS PUBLISHED BY
HEART'S DISCOVERY:

All Titles by SG Williams are Available on Amazon:

Victoria Hall: Secrets, Rumours & Hauntings –
Feb. 4 2024

Colours of The Light: Stories and Lessons for our
Times – Oct. 31 2023

RiseUp3 – Oct. 14 2023

The Code for Empowered Healing: For Ourselves
& Our Planet – Jan. 25 2023

The Art of Getting Younger: Beyond Healing –
April 30 2022

Reflections: Poetry & Prose about Everyday life –
July 5 2021

Too Close For Comfort: Escape from a Destructive
Cult – June 27 2021

Love's Call To Madness: A Personal Journey –
April 1 2021

Our Rightful Place in Health & Happiness: Healing
Insights – Jan. 30 2021